The Blessings of Unity

The Blessings of Unity
God's Best for Our Marriages

Richard T Case

elevate

Scripture quotations taken from the New American Standard Bible®,
Copyright © 1960, 1962, 1963, 1968, 1971, 1972, 1973,
1975, 1977, 1995 by The Lockman Foundation
Used by permission. (www.Lockman.org)

Editorial Content: AnnaMarie McHargue and Dave Troesh
Cover Designer: Arthur Cherry

Published by Elevate Publishing, Boise, ID www.elevatepub.com

Printed in the United States of America
ISBN 13: 9781943425105

Contents

Introduction

My wife, Linda, and I have been doing marriage retreats for over 14 years. We have been quite amazed and rather shocked at the state of Christian marriages today. Recent statistics show that between 50 and 60 percent of all Christian marriages wind up in divorce, the same percentage as unbelievers. Of the marriages that have not moved to divorce, we find only a few that are truly reflecting the glory and wonder of God. Sadly, most couples are living in mediocrity, on-going conflict, and certainly not enjoying the beauty of the institution of marriage. We find several causes for this:

1. Men and women are attracted to each other because of their differences in personalities. God made us in this fashion as we were always intended to complete each other through these differences. However, in today's society, because of our tendency to self-centeredness, these natural differences in personalities become irritants and cause great friction in the marriage. The husband is trying to force the wife to become more like him while the wife is forcing the husband to become more like her. Since fundamental personality cannot be altered, these attempts to change characteristics do not work and result in significant conflicts—ultimately creating deep levels of anger and bitterness.

1

2. Most are operating in the flesh, not walking in the spirit, and are normally self-centered, and thus two people that are self-centered will experience difficulty. Each will want their own way and work hard to persuade the other of their own way—willing to go to battle to get their own way.

3. There happens to be very little teaching on what is it means for a husband to love his wife as Christ so loves the church; and thus the conclusion is just for wives to submit. This issue of a wife's submission is found in Ephesians Chapter 5. While there is an important element that is described in Ephesians, it is taken out of context because it doesn't reflect all of Ephesians in the truths of Ephesians. As a result some Christian marriages are being operated in a way that is actually not of God. Husbands rarely love their wives as Christ loves the church; but they do ask their wives to be submissive to their decisions. Consequently, wives have seen the fallacy and the failures of these decisions, and develop deep levels of anger and bitterness. It leads them to not trust their husbands and to work at establishing a life of their own outside of the marriage. There is general sadness, oppression, and lack of joy in their marriages and families. This can lead further to the decision for separation and divorce, since neither party sees much hope for happiness or long-lasting love in their futures.

4. In today's materialistic world, both the husband and wife are working, attempting to establish a level of income that can maintain their desired standard of living. They find this norm more difficult, especially with the current economic times of high unemployment and lower wages. Furthermore, there is high credit card debt and high mortgages relative to the value of their homes. This

creates extreme financial pressure, which causes even more conflict in the marriage, especially when there are not agreements on budgets, financial condition, and planning for the future. There is very little safety net being developed by most marriages. Thus the fear of being laid off (which is more and more likely these days) weighs heavily on the emotional life of a marriage.

5. In today's world, our children are bombarded with extraordinary peer pressure along with cultural stressors such as drugs, alcohol, sex, being accepted, and the gay agenda. They lack a solid social environment due to their self-absorption into video games and entertainment. Raising children has become a most difficult proposition. Many husbands and wives do not spend the energy to shepherd their children properly (usually because work is so predominant in their life) and certainly, they are not in agreement about how to shepherd their children. As a result the normal conflicts between a husband and wife are being exacerbated by the conflicts within the family and thus the failures that are being experienced in the family.

The sexual life of a marriage is ordained by God and given as a source of great enjoyment. However, because of emotional conflict, weariness, stubbornness, and lack of care, many couples' sexual life has degraded to perfunctory levels with little pleasure. While the reasons for affairs are deeper than lack of sexual enjoyment in a partner, it certainly contributes to the thinking that having an affair is acceptable and even justifiable. Working in the marketplace, where there are both men and women, has created an environment where connections with the opposite sex outside of the marriage are readily available and these relationships can easily develop into affairs. Furthermore, social media sites like Facebook create another environment for connection and the potential for physical connection. This once again creates a short-term level of acceptance of satisfaction instead of a long-term commitment to marriage.

Perhaps underlying all of these is the sad truth that, neither the husband nor the wife, is spending time abiding with Christ. They do not have vital spiritual walks on their own and certainly not together—mostly because they have not learned how. The church is failing miserably at teaching this critical relationship-developing truth. Further, we have found that church attendance is not regular and is not fully satisfying to the marriage or the family. They are not receiving the depth of the Word nor challenged to go deeper into the Word themselves. As a result, they are not experiencing the vital life of the Spirit. By operating in the flesh, in the natural, there can be no movement into the beauty and the fullness of God's life for the marriage.

6. Linda and I discovered the solution to all of this as we grew in our marriage. We had experienced similar difficulties because we were operating in the same way that many of the above issues are described. We recognized that something wasn't right and that there had to be truth and understanding that could alter how we were functioning as a Christian couple before God. We learned that there are two keys to successful marriages—each of us must:

    1. Be abiding in the Vine and walking in the Spirit. (John 15: 1–15)

    2. Learning the concept of unity—we are to live and only live through the principle of unity. This means working toward reaching agreement on all decisions, all issues, and all things of our lives 100 percent of the time, all the time. (Psalm 133)

This book will walk through the Biblical truths of these two keys, illustrating how they will lead all of us to exceptional, outstanding, superb marriages—God's true plan for us.

As a premise, we set forth the following verses:

Psalm 133:1
Behold, how good and pleasant it is for brethren to dwell together in unity...for there the Lord commands the blessing:

It clearly states that it is good and pleasant to dwell (live out in everyday life) in unity with those close to us (most importantly our spouses). The Words in the Hebrew here mean: *good:* pleasant, agreeable (to the senses); pleasant (to our higher nature), excellent, rich, valuable in estimation, glad, happy, prosperous; **pleasant:** delightful, sweet, lovely, agreeable; **dwell:** remain in: **unity:** union, united-ness, agreement, oneness; **commanded:** ordered: **blessing:** gifts, prosperity.

When we reach unity together in Christ (through abiding) we discover His will, walk with Him into this will, and there He COMMANDS BLESSING. Remember, it is not negotiation or compromise, but rather, seeking together with another like-minded partner or friend (who also is abiding) what God speaks and desires—true unity. Why would we not then go to unity? We will show that the answer is, of course we would go to unity "for there, God commands His blessing." Blessing will happen. It will be so. It will be the best and none better. It will be fantastic. It will be exceptional. It will be superb. Why would we not then live in unity?

CHAPTER 1
Evaluation of Your Marriage

Each SPOUSE should write out the current big decisions you are facing. Include all the current issues and on-going areas of conflict/disagreement in your marriage. What questions do you have regarding God's will for any of these? You should each do this exercise separately and then come together to compare notes. See what is common and what is unique. See if you can agree on the list and then work to prioritize the list; first in importance, second, third, etc. Do not, at the moment, attempt to resolve any issues. Just agree that you both accept that these are the things in your lives right now that you are truly facing. Keep these in the forefront as you go through the book; and use these issues as practice to bring these truths into real, practical application for you.

Now, each spouse separately rate the characteristics of Unity in your marriage; on a scale of 1—5, 1 being best and couldn't be better, 5 being awful and could not be worse. Be honest and make the evaluation based upon what you truly think and feel right now in your marriage—how things really are operating now:

Husband:
Level of Unity with spouse

1   2   3   4   5

What is your Spouse's Ability to Process?
Ability to listen

1   2   3   4   5

Ability to share emotions/feelings

1   2   3   4   5

Encouraging you to share emotions/feelings

1   2   3   4   5

Not getting defensive during discussion

1   2   3   4   5

Willingness to change position (not stubborn)

1   2   3   4   5

Ability to discuss calmly vs. argue/debate

1   2   3   4   5

Ability to discuss creative solutions

1   2   3   4   5

Ability to enjoy your day even in the middle of disagreement/difference of opinion

1   2   3   4   5

What is your spouse's desire to seek the will of God with you?

1   2   3   4   5

Desire/frequency to pray together and seek God's will?

1   2   3   4   5

Desire/frequency to be in the Word together as you seek God's will?

1   2   3   4   5

Wife:
Level of Unity with spouse

   1   2   3   4   5

What is your Spouse's Ability to Process?
Ability to listen

   1   2   3   4   5

Ability to share emotions/feelings

   1   2   3   4   5

Encouraging you to share emotions/feelings

   1   2   3   4   5

Not getting defensive during discussion

   1   2   3   4   5

Willingness to change position (not stubborn)

   1   2   3   4   5

Ability to discuss calmly vs. argue/debate

   1   2   3   4   5

Ability to discuss creative solutions

   1   2   3   4   5

Ability to enjoy your day even in the middle of disagreement/difference of opinion

   1   2   3   4   5

What is your spouse's desire to seek the will of God with you?

   1   2   3   4   5

Desire/frequency to pray together and seek God's will?

   1   2   3   4   5

Desire/frequency to be in the Word together as you seek God's will?

   1   2   3   4   5

Now, discuss these ratings with each other and explain your reasoning. Do not let these become a source of conflict or irritation. Simply use the data to establish the truth of the status of your marriage and relationship to facilitate being able to pursue unity. If you both agree that an item is rated low then it might be one to focus on utilizing the processes presented in this book. If your spouse has rated something low and the other spouse rated it high, it still should be considered an issue. The reality of that perception means that there truly is something that needs to be addressed. Also keep this item in mind as you work through the book.

One of the key aspects that you will learn about unity is going to truth, pursuing truth, and seeking truth together. This evaluation is simply to establish the baseline for the truth of your marriage at this moment. Do not consider it to be good or bad but rather that it is what it is. Based upon this, you will be able to see where the Lord would transform your hearts and begin to reveal His new truth. This will allow you to together see that unity will provide God's way of understanding His will, which is going to be best and none better; the most blessed place to be, especially since He commands blessings there.

CHAPTER 2

Division and Discord—
the Opposite of Unity

What is division/discord (opposite of unity) and what are its consequences?

In order to truly understand unity in God's view of unity, let's look at its opposite, division and discord. We need to fully understand the consequences of not pursuing unity and thus, living in division and discord. As we come to truly understand these consequences, we will have a strong motivation to never allow division and discord to be characteristic of our marriages. Instead, we will always have a strong desire to seek unity.

> *Proverbs 6: 16–19:*
> *16 These six things the Lord hates, Yes, seven are an abomination to Him: 17 A proud look, A lying tongue, Hands that shed innocent blood, 18 A heart that devises wicked plans, Feet that are swift in running to evil, 19 A false witness who speaks lies, And one who sows discord among brethren.*

It is clear and simple—God hates division. The word here, division (or discord) means strife, contention and judging others. God calls division an abomination—something

detestable to Him—actually disgusting—very strong statements in the Hebrew. If God hates division and finds it disgusting, then so should we. We should realize that when we're living
in division we cannot be pleasing Him.

> ### Romans 8: 5–8:
> 5 *For those who live according to the flesh set their minds*
> *on the things of the flesh, but those who live according to*
> *the Spirit, the things of the Spirit. 6 For to be carnally*
> *minded is death, but to be spiritually minded is life and*
> *peace. 7 Because the carnal mind is enmity against God;*
> *for it is not subject to the law of God, nor indeed can be.*
> *8 So then, those who are in the flesh cannot please God.*

Division is primarily caused by us living in the flesh—allowing self-centeredness—and not walking in the Spirit. When we,
as believers, are living in the flesh, there are three serious consequences to our lives:

1. **We put to death the very Spirit that has been given
   us by the Father.** Even though we still have the spirit
   residing within us, we, in essence, are putting the life of
   the Spirit to death. The Greek word here means walking
   without the Light in the thickest darkness—on our own
   and away from the protection and life of the Spirit. We
   are basically reliving what Adam and Eve experienced in
   the Garden of Eden when they died. They lost the Holy
   Spirit and were left with just material flesh and soul.
   The soul is the essence of who we are—our personality,
   our will, our intellect and our emotions. Animals also
   have material flesh and soul. When a man or woman
   operates absent of the Holy Spirit, they are actually
   just sophisticated animals. They are superior in intellect but living the same way as animals—self-centered,

self-agenda, self-preservation and self-directed. The import to us in our marriage is that if we are operating in the flesh, then we are self-centered which will naturally lead to division and discord. Each partner will go to battle to achieve their own way—all because, in essence, they have put to death the life of the Spirit.

2. **We place ourselves at enmity against God.** While seeking our own way instead of cooperating and pursuing God's will we actually fight against and oppose God's will.. We are not sensitive to His invitation to walk with Him and to experience His will, which is nothing but good for us. Instead, we resist His will and experience the consequences of not walking in His will. This creates an interesting paradox. We suffer negative consequences which are difficult, frustrating, hard and troublesome. Since we think that God is in complete control of our lives we believe that we should not experience these negative consequences. As a result, we blame God. This causes us to further seek our own way since we do not believe that He is going to act on our best behalf. The paradox is that we believe God is at enmity against us when in reality we are at enmity against Him. We are simply suffering the consequences of being at enmity against Him. He is always for us and always desires to have us live in His kingdom and experience the wonder of His beautiful will. However, because we are deciding to live in the flesh, we place ourselves outside of His kingdom and thus suffer the consequences especially since we are at enmity against Him.

3. **We cannot please Him.** Even if we are active in church, attending church, doing ministry, leading Bible studies—because we are living in the flesh, we will not be

able to please Him. It is not about what we are doing for Him but rather the life that He is giving us as we walk with Him. This life is the Spirit life which will be able to lead us into unity and into His will. If we please Him we will be able to experience this life. If we cannot please Him, because we walk in the flesh, we will not be able to experience this life or His will.

James 4:11:

11 Do not speak evil of one another, brethren. He who speaks evil of a brother and judges his brother, speaks evil of the law and judges the law. But if you judge the law, you are not a doer of the law but a judge.

This addresses an interesting truth regarding our marriages. James 4:11 says that if we judge each other we are actually speaking evil to each other. Here, the word judge means that we have pronounced our opinion as being right; and our spouse's opinion as being wrong. We are actually speaking against the one we love. We've already decided that we are correct. We therefore judge the other person and work to persuade them to accept what we've decided is right. We have actually moved into judgment and are speaking evil.

James 5: 9:

9 Do not grumble against one another, brethren, lest you be condemned. Behold, the Judge is standing at the door!

This says that as we grumble, complain and work to persuade the other party that we are right, and them wrong, we bring condemnation onto ourselves. We who have judged others (i.e. prematurely established that we are right and the other party wrong) and condemn them are actually bringing condemnation upon ourselves. The righteousness and holiness of God automatically condemns us because our hearts have moved toward self-righteousness to establish our position as God and not surrendered to God.

Galatians 5: 1–4:

1 Stand fast therefore in the liberty by which Christ has made us free, and do not be entangled again with a yoke of bondage. 2 Indeed I, Paul, say to you that if you become circumcised, Christ will profit you nothing. 3 And I testify again to every man who becomes circumcised that he is a debtor to keep the whole law. 4 You have become estranged from Christ, you who attempt to be justified by law; you have fallen from grace.

These verses explain the precise consequences of going to judgment against our spouse. It brings condemnation upon our self. It first urges us to no longer be entangled in bondage (be enslaved) to this process of judgment—as it will not go well for us (not profit us—have no value). It clearly states that if we bring one element of judgment against our spouse (I am right and she/he is wrong.), we are bringing the entire law against us and are thus obligated to keep the entire law—an interesting truth of judgment. We cannot just decide that one rule or what we think to be right is okay—it elevates automatically that all the law must then be followed—and we know that our ability to keep the entire law is nil. As a result we have serious consequences:

1. **We become estranged from Christ.** We actually separate ourselves from the life of Christ and no longer have access to the spiritual power or the life that He provides. This word "estranged" here means we deprive ourselves of the power and life of the Spirit—actually cause it to cease and pass away.

2. **We fall from grace**. The Greek word here for "grace" means joy, pleasure, delight, sweetness, charm, loveliness, grace of speech, good will, loving-kindness, favor. So, we actually have moved out of and lose the favor of God and will suffer the negative consequences of living in the world outside of the protection and favor of God.

So what does all this mean? If we establish our position as right and are working to persuade our spouse that they are wrong, we are bringing judgment upon our self. We will be experiencing the serious consequences of being separated from Christ and have fallen from the favor of God—no wonder we are struggling in life so much! This is a critical piece of the process to understand. It is not our right to bring judgment but rather to pursue truth together. This does not mean that we don't have disagreement or can't see things differently. Rather, it means that we don't come at our disagreements with a heart that thinks I'm right and the other person is wrong and it's my job to persuade them. The better way is to believe that I'm right but I'm willing to process truth to see God's truth and thus not come into judgment or condemnation.

> *Genesis 13: 6–7:*
> *6 Now the land was not able to support them, that they might dwell together, for their possessions were so great that they could not dwell together. 7 And there was strife between the herdsmen of Abram's livestock and the herdsmen of Lot's livestock. The Canaanites and the Perizzites then dwelt in the land.*

This is an interesting little story about Abraham and Lot. They were family and moving from place to place together with their flocks and herds, as directed by the Spirit. God prospered their entire family and their flocks and herds increased significantly.

Because the available land became too small to occupy with all of the increased herds and flocks, Lot and Abraham began to argue about who had the rights to the land. They went to strife—harsh quarreling. As a result of this division, they split apart and separated. So, instead of working together to manage their prosperity and remain as a family, they looked only at what was theirs and fought over it—separating the family physically and more importantly emotionally. This is characteristic of a lot of marriages and families. They are blessed with many material things and wind up arguing and debating about these material things—particularly where couples have set up "this is yours" and "this is mine" and they never have completely combined their financials or material things together. What God provided as blessing turns into difficulty and stress, causing great conflict, anger, and frustration as they fight and argue over the very stuff of life. Think about how totally absurd this is.

Acts 15: 36–40:
35 Paul and Barnabas also remained in Antioch, teaching and preaching the word of the Lord, with many others also. 36 Then after some days Paul said to Barnabas, "Let us now go back and visit our brethren in every city where we have preached the word of the Lord, and see how they are doing." 37 Now Barnabas was determined to take with them John called Mark. 38 But Paul insisted that they should not take with them the one who had departed from them in Pamphylia, and had not gone with them to the work. 39 Then the contention became so sharp that they parted from one another. And so Barnabas took Mark and sailed to Cyprus; 40 but Paul chose Silas and departed, being commended by the brethren to the grace of God.

This is another interesting story of conflict. Paul and Barnabas had become best of friends as they labored in ministry together.

When Paul was first converted in Damascus, Barnabas was the one that befriended him, listened to what had happened, and stood up for him before the apostles to verify that the conversion was real. Paul left Barnabas and went home to Tarsus where he poured through the Old Testament and gained new insight and revelation of the truths of the Scriptures in light of what Christ did for us on the cross and resurrection—and his new revelation in the Spirit became the basis of much of the New Testament for us. While he was growing in his understanding, the gospel had spread to Antioch, a Gentile community north of Israel, where many converts came to know Christ and were gathering together as a church. Knowing that they needed leadership, the Jerusalem Council sent Barnabas to shepherd this flock.

While Barnabus was there the new church experienced such growth that its needs exceeded his abilities and capacity (he wisely understood the priesthood of the believer as the church was never intended to be a single pastor model, but a sharing of the church ministry through all the gifts given to all believers). As a result, he remembered this fellow called Saul who was converted and traveled to Tarsus and asked him to join him in this work, which he did. They stayed there together ministering—as Barnabas was discipling not only the leaders of Antioch but also Paul himself.

While at Antioch, the Holy Spirit called Barnabas and Paul to go on a journey (called the first missionary journey)—to spread the gospel and "raise up" church leaders in other Gentile communities. Barnabas, due to his leadership experience, was selected as the leader of the group. During the journey where the gospel was exploding and churches were being developed, Barnabas recognized Saul's leadership, intellectual and spiritual abilities (and given a new name of Paul) and placed him in leadership. They returned to Antioch after a successful missionary trip, and stayed there together ministering—experiencing the wonderful works of God and continuing to enjoy their friendship together. When a conflict arose over circumcision (we will discuss this later), the church sent Paul and Barnabas to Jerusalem to bring clarity and unity to this division, which they did. Through this, they learned the key principles of processing disagreement. Afterwards, the Holy Spirit again called Paul and Barnabas to go on another missionary journey (called the second missionary journey), since they had such a close relationship and were so effective together.

It was at this point that Paul stubbornly refused to include John Mark. Due to fear and homesickness, John Mark had abandoned Paul and Barnabas on the first missionary journey. Barnabas disagreed with Paul, and even though he understood why Paul would think that way, he saw the great Spiritual potential in John Mark. Barnabas had already gone to forgiveness of John Mark and felt that he deserved a second chance to experience the power of God on their next missionary trip. There arose such a sharp disagreement, primarily because Paul was not willing to consider anyone else's view other than his own. It became so contentious that Paul took a dogmatic position and refused to allow John Mark to go with them—even being so stubborn that he was willing to stand on this position at the cost of destroying his deep friendship with Barnabas. Barnabas knew that this was not God's will and thus could not, before God, continue with Paul on his second missionary journey. So, Barnabas took John Mark with him back to Barnabas' home town in Cyprus and continued to disciple him there. Paul took Silas and went on the second missionary journey. The journey was again successful but we will never know the fullness of what might have happened had Paul and Barnabas desired to go to unity in this particular disagreement. They certainly broke friendship over it and lost the beauty of that relationship from that point forward. The good news is that Paul later on recognized that Barnabas was correct and that Paul's stubbornness was not. In 2 Timothy 4:11, the last book that Paul wrote, he asked Luke to bring John Mark back with them because he was most valuable for his ministry. Furthermore John Mark is the author of the gospel of Mark. We see that Barnabas's view was actually God's will and later Paul recognized it as well. It was unfortunate that the sharp disagreement caused two good friends to no longer live out the relationship that characterized the power of co-laboring in Christ. Even spouses and good friends can separate (if not physically than emotionally) over strong disagreements where either party become intransient and stubborn in their view, and there is not and a willingness to pursue truth and God's will. It ends in division and discord.

My wife (of 45 years now) and I were high school sweethearts. We got married when I was 20 and Linda was 18. In those days (the good ole days) a male had to be 21 years old to get a marriage license so this required my parents to sign for me. I was then a junior in college at Bradley University in Peoria, Illinois; Linda was a freshman there. Our first summer of being married we lived in an apartment in Valparaiso, Indiana where I grew up. We were both working. We were in love, enjoyed being together, and since we had no money, not much worried us. Our big treat in Valparaiso was to get a a 25-cent dipped Dairy Queen ice cream cone and go to the Indiana Dunes beach. We had a very fun summer. We both then went back to Bradley University where I graduated early, at the end of the first semester. Knowing that I wanted to get an MBA, I applied to many schools; and was hoping to go to Harvard. However, the University only admitted a new entrant in the fall so I would have had to wait eight months to attend. I knew that had I gone directly to work, I probably would never go back to school. So I chose USC in California, which did allow mid-year entrance. We packed everything we owned in our Camaro and drove west.

The second day we were there, we experienced the 6.8 Sylmar earthquake. Being from the Midwest, we had heard that a major earthquake would cause California to fall into the ocean. Our apartment happened to be next to a pool, and during the earthquake we heard a huge slap of water against our walls—we thought this is it, we have fallen into the ocean. To say the least, it was an interesting introduction to California. After a few months of graduate school, we discovered that Linda was pregnant. In those days it was normal to have the wife stay at home with the baby while the husband went to work. Thus, I knew I had to probably quit school and get to work. However, I inquired of the Dean if I could do a fast track by taking exams for material though not able to attend the classes, so that I could get through early. He allowed me this privilege, and I finished my MBA in seven months, one week after our daughter was born.

We moved to Long Beach and I began my career. Having the baby and working full-time certainly changed the dynamics of our lives. Up to that point, we had lived a relaxed life, enjoyed our first year of marriage, the adventures of Valparaiso, finishing college and moving to California for my Masters. Because I was ambitious and had a dream of becoming an executive, I poured my life into my work. I basically worked six days a week, 10 to 12 hours a day including the long California commutes. I rarely saw our daughter, and spent little time with Linda. She was struggling, learning how to raise a new baby, and I was basically absent—trying to get ahead. That was the beginning of our years of dissension and division. We both had strong personalities, but mine was stronger. I was gifted with a great memory that can remember facts, and the ability to use logic to prove my point. No matter what Linda would present, I could talk around it and proved my point until she finally gave in, since she had nowhere else to go with her position. I won arguments—my goal. I believed that I was right and she was wrong and that she needed to do what I thought was right. Though she could not overtly win arguments, she would be passive-aggressive and was developing a level of resentment for not being honored. Our marriage was characterized by irritation and weekly arguments—which I always won.

Later we moved to Mission Viejo and since we had a baby thought it wise to attend church. We went to Presbyterian Church of the Master and signed the guest card. They sent a team out to our house that was practicing Kennedy's Evangelism Explosion (EE). The program is intended to ask specific questions including: if you died tonight, on what basis would you be allowed to get into heaven? Most people share that they are pretty good and that certainly God allows all good people to enter into heaven. They then explain that we all have a sin nature, fall short of the requirements of God (perfection) and thus need a solution. That solution is Christ who gave himself for us and died on the cross, was resurrected and now offers us this life, having taken the penalty required (atonement). That night, the team that visited included two businessmen and a businessman's wife who had not seen each other in a month but were quite good friends. They came in and started sharing with each other the excitement of all that Christ had done through answered prayer. They were so excited, that they basically forgot about Linda and I. After 45 minutes of enthusiastic sharing, they said that they had to return home and would call us later. They never asked us any questions. However, their sharing about Christ was something that really struck our hearts. Linda and I discussed how we were missing that dynamic in our life and wanted to experience it as well. So we got down on our knees by our bed and prayed that God would give us what they had. A few days later they called us and inviting us to dinner. We discussed what we had prayed for and they shared Christ with us and we received Him together as our Lord and Savior. They asked us if we wanted to start a couples' Bible study to learn what the Word has to speak to us. We said sure. So every Friday night we would gather together and over the next two years this group grew to be approximately 50 couples. We would all bring our children who would sleep in this huge room with sleeping bags and we would stay up until midnight or later diving into the Word and learning what it has to say. This was quite inspirational.

Through this time, I learned that I needed to have a more balanced approach to work and family and to enjoy Linda and the family more. Though our relationship improved, I still dominated our decisions and still won every argument. We had an ongoing level of dissension and disunity, because we knew no better. Our life was okay and interesting, but our relationship drifted because of this dissension. All the Christians around us were living in similar fashion, and they all stated that this was normal—just try to do our best. Our best was pretty weak, and we drifted as most couples do into mediocrity where our lives were "just getting by." We had no power in our lives. We guessed that our lives were as good as they could be.

What are the Primary Causes of Division/Discord?

Galatians 5: 17: Galatians 5: 19–21; 26:
17 For the flesh lusts against the Spirit, and the Spirit against the flesh; and these are contrary to one another, so that you do not do the things that you wish...19 Now the works of the flesh are evident, which are: adultery, fornication, uncleanness, lewdness, 20 idolatry, sorcery, hatred, contentions, jealousies, outbursts of wrath, selfish ambitions, dissensions, heresies, 21 envy, murders, drunkenness, revelries, and the like; of which I tell you beforehand, just as I also told you in times past, that those who practice such things will not inherit the kingdom of God. ...26 Let us not become conceited, provoking one another, envying one another.

The primary cause of division and discord is selfishness. As believers, we are still faced with the ongoing battle of the flesh against the spirit—and these are completely contrary to each other. Since we have this ongoing battle, our lives will be characterized by which force is dominating the battle. The flesh takes us back to selfishness where we exercise our self will, pursue our self agenda, and are willing to fight over what we believe we want and what we think is right. As a result, we fail knowing that we would like to do we can't do; things that we know we shouldn't do we do. This translates into a list of characteristics that are completely opposing God:

- Adultery
- Fornication
- Uncleanness
- Lewdness
- Idolatry
- Sorcery
- Hatred (deep anger)
- Contentions
- Jealousies
- Outburst of wrath
- Selfish ambitions
- Dissensions
- Heresies
- Envy
- Murders
- Drunkenness
- Revelries

As you can see, all the items on this list are reflective of deep self-centeredness that translates into breaking relationships, emotional distress, deep anger, contention and dissension, and basically hardness and separation within our relationship(s). The Scriptures here tell us that Christians who are operating in such a way cannot inherit the kingdom of God. The power and the wonder of the kingdom that is available to us will not be operating in our lives. We will be functioning as practical atheists, outside the protection and beauty of God's kingdom of righteousness, peace and joy. Another severe consequence is that we wind up actually stimulating the other party to move into the flesh as well. This only exacerbates the level of conflict that we will be experiencing.

This leads us to the consequences of Romans 8: 5–8

> *5 For those who live according to the flesh set their minds on the things of the flesh, but those who live according to the Spirit, the things of the Spirit. 6 For to be carnally minded is death, but to be spiritually minded is life and peace. 7 Because the carnal mind is enmity against God; for it is not subject to the law of God, nor indeed can be. 8 So then, those who are in the flesh cannot please God.*

If the flesh is dominating, we are then setting our mind on the things of the flesh and allowing the seventeen consequences of the flesh, listed above, to characterize our lives. This is because we are living in the flesh, have put to death the life of the Spirit, become at enmity against God and cannot please him. Our lives are thus characterized by strife in contention which only goes deeper as we then tend to blame God for the difficulties that we are experiencing—believing that He is at enmity against us when in fact He is quite the opposite.

Which leads us to James 4: 1–4:

> *1 Where do wars and fights come from among you? Do they not come from your desires for pleasure that war in your members? 2 You lust and do not have. You murder and covet and cannot obtain. You fight and war. Yet you do not have because you do not ask. 3 You ask and do not receive, because you ask amiss, that you may spend it on your pleasures. 4 Adulterers and adulteresses! Do you not*

know that friendship with the world is enmity with God?
Whoever therefore wants to be a friend of the world makes
himself an enemy of God.

While we are operating in the flesh, we experience many quarrels and arguments—even war where we are working to hurt the other party. Scripture tells us here that the reason for these is our self-centeredness. As a result of this self-centeredness, we actually stop praying. We no longer ask God to reveal "Himself and His will," or for Him to resolve the issues of our life. More profoundly, in our self-centeredness we often are still praying, but not experiencing any answers. The reason is that we are asking amiss—asking for what we would like to have happen and for God to support our self-centeredness. He cannot answer these prayers because He cannot allow us to serve as God and to relegate Him to become our Genie, serving our self-interest. So our marriages are characterized by lack of prayer, weak self-centered prayer, and little experience of the life of God. This causes us to spiral even deeper into self-centeredness and farther into conflict. We have little spiritual vitality and develop deeper levels of resentment toward each other. Ultimately, we start to resent God since we do not understand why our prayers are not being answered and blame Him for not caring about us.

It is not complicated to see that God hates dissension and that dissension leads us into a life of stress and oppression. As we slip farther and farther into the flesh, we either: stop praying or pray selfishly and never experience the fullness of the kingdom of God. We need to fully comprehend that this is not God's will for our lives. We need not be living in constant disagreement with our spouses, and that there is a better way for us to live—God's way.

It is important to understand that division and discord should be as much an abomination to us as it is to God. We must see that going to judgment (through prematurely deciding that we are right and the other party is wrong) leads us to operating in the flesh, where we put to death the life of the Spirit, are at enmity against God, and cannot please Him. Further, this separates us from the vital relationship in Christ and we have fallen from the favor of God. It should be clear that division is one of the key reasons that things do not go well for us and is the cause of unhappiness and conflict. Thus we are called to make a choice. Decide not to let conflict and discord characterize our relationships, but rather to work together to experience the fullness of the life of God through the Spirit. Rather than discord, we are called to learn to go to unity.

Throughout the next years of our marriage and family, we experienced many ups and downs. Though we were Christians, we were never taught that we still had a basic choice in life— to either walk in the Spirit or by default, walk in the selfishness of the flesh. . Since we had no understanding of the Spirit life, we were selfish. We both wanted our own way and fought each other to get our own way. I did it by winning arguments and dominating decisions. Linda did it by getting back at me through use of credit cards and withdrawal from sex. Though we were selfish, we thought this normal and just lived with the state of tension. Our life was okay and we experienced many good things. Unfortunately, we battled over many of the everyday decisions involving finances, raising children and family dynamics. We moved from California to Corning New York where I became an executive for Corning Glass Works. It was quite a wonderful time of growing as an executive at Fortune 500 company and we certainly enjoyed the beauty of upstate New York. We had a very nice house and were able to travel to many new places on the East Coast. As a young believer, I became zealous for evangelism and decided that being in the business world was evil and that I instead should become a pastor. We left Corning where our life was reasonably stable and went to seminary at Trinity Evangelical Divinity School in Chicago. Since I wanted to get through school as quickly as possible, I took 20-plus hours a quarter of classes. I also took on the role of pastor of a failing church in North side of Chicago near Wrigley Field. It was a liberal church, but because I was an executive and willing to serve for minimal pay ($300/month plus a parsonage) the church hired me. Because I was now a full-time pastor and an over full-time student, I never had time to see our two daughters or Linda. I told her that we were serving God and to "suck it up, and put up with this difficult life." Linda was dying emotionally and getting sadder and sadder. Division and dissension were the norm—but my dominance prevailed over anything that she thought or felt.

One day, I was invited to attend a CBMC (The Christian Business Men's Committee) luncheon. The president of the organization walked over to me and said that God had told him to get to know me and Linda, and invited us to his house. When we arrived, he asked me to share about our life. I told him and his wife about how I had given up a career in business, was zealously serving God and the church, going to school and was doing all of this for minimal financial income. He leaned across the table and said, "What a bunch of crap. I did not hear you speak of your lovely wife here and your marriage or your children and family. You have missed entirely what is God's will for your life. You don't know anything about walking with God. Would you like to learn how?" Linda said, "Yes, he would."

Over the next several months this couple discipled Linda and I on how to seek God's will and make decisions that were in line with His will for our lives. I completed seminary, but left the church as pastor. Then, I went to work for American Hospital Supply Corporation, another Fortune 500 company. We enjoyed a more balanced life and our marriage improved. However, we had not dealt with the root cause of division— selfishness. Though I was a better husband, I still dominated our decisions and won every debate and argument. I thought

I was more spiritual, but really just operated at a deeper selfish level to get what I wanted.

One big series of decisions dramatically impacted our life. Though a senior executive for a Fortune 500 company at a young age (29), I was advised that investing in real estate was an excellent way to gain equity. Through research, I determined that Dallas, Texas was the easiest place to invest. So, with a few investors, bought a commercial plot, built a building, leased the building and then sold the building—all over a two year period. We made in excess of $1 million profit. It seemed so easy. I calculated that by investing just a few hours each week, I could do three buildings that would create incredible wealth over the next decade. Linda said that she did not feel right in her spirit about that strategy, and urged me to not proceed. As usual, I won the debate and proved that my strategy was correct—what could go wrong?

Well, it did go wrong. I hit the late 70s early 80s recession and I, along with multiple other builders of office buildings, had empty office buildings. In a downturn businesses do not grow, they shrink and thus do not add space. The interest on the loans had to be paid, and I ran out of capability to pay. The banks required that I file Chapter 7 and give back the buildings. I lost all of my stock equity in the company that I worked for, all of our savings and the investor's money as well. The day that we filed bankruptcy, my automobiles were taken away on a truck and we literally had zero dollars in all of our bank accounts. In the bankruptcy, everything that we owned was considered an asset and thus I had to buy back all of our furniture and all of Linda's jewelry—including her wedding ring. The judge allowed me to pay for this over time—but we had lost everything; all due to my selfishness and unwillingness to process decisions in unity. I thought I was spiritual, but really was carnal, and certainly had no idea about going to unity with Linda. Having failed so miserably, I was about to learn.

CHAPTER 3
Unity

As opposed to the life of the flesh that leads to self-centeredness, contentions, deep anger, separation, stress and frustration, God offers us a life of the Spirit. His life brings about beauty, wonder, peace, joy, love, excitement and the supernatural works of God. And interestingly enough, a key gateway into this kingdom life is unity. In the Scriptures this word is defined as agreement, being in harmony, being in unison, seeing things the same way, walking together, and living as one. And for believers, this unity is not just between my spouse and I, but rather my spouse, me and God. And since God is the vinedresser, all-powerful, all-knowing and all-present, when we reach unity with Him, we reach the best and none better.

What is Unity and what are its blessings?

Ecclesiastes 4: 9–12:
9 Two are better than one; Because they have a good reward for their labor. 10 For if they fall, one will lift up his companion. But woe to him who is alone when he falls, For he has no one to help him up. 11 Again, if two lie down together, they will keep warm; But how can one be warm alone? 12 Though one may be overpowered by another, two can withstand him. And a threefold cord is not quickly broken.

Ecclesiastes tells us that two are better (the Greek word here is the same word as good: pleasant, agreeable to senses, excellent, rich, valuable, glad, happy, prosperous—the Best!!) than one—because of these key reasons:

1. When one of us falls the other one is there to lift us up.

2. When one is cold (struggling), being together warms (comforts) both.

3. When we experience opposition (particularly spiritual opposition) two are able to stand against it whereas one alone cannot.

In essence, we are to be each other's best cheerleader with an objective of being there for each other, particularly when there's struggle, opposition, difficulty, and feelings of loneliness. The Scripture goes on to tell us that a threefold cord cannot be broken. God is lifting the concept of the two of us walking together supporting and encouraging each other with the thought of uniting with God where nothing can break us, pull us apart, or prevail against us. We will always have different things come at us at different times. If we are operating in a self-centered way, we actually intensify the difficulty by requesting, if not demanding our partner change their behavior and solve their own problems. But God says two (and really three with Him) are better than one because nothing will be able to overcome us, and the frustrations of life can be released. It is important to settle this—that two are better than one; but in unity with Him and we will stand even stronger together. Thus, when our partner is struggling, we should approach the struggle differently. Rather than exacerbate their burden and intensify their frustration, we are called to support our spouse in a deeper way. We are to help our spouse understand the spiritual dynamic, then help them reconnect to the Vine in abiding and let the Spirit bring answers and healing. Our heart will develop a more caring emotion, and will demonstrate to our spouse that we are their best cheerleader and always want them to experience the fullness of God's life. We will thus do anything to help them through this and be there for them. Two are better than one.

Genesis 2: 24–25:
24 Therefore a man shall leave his father and mother and be joined to his wife, and they shall become one flesh. 25 And they were both naked, the man and his wife, and were not ashamed.

Genesis tells us that we are to leave our father and mother and cleave together (stay close, join to, stick with) with our spouse—joining to become one (be in unity and agreement, always). This instruction was given to Adam and Eve (who did not have a mother and father), before the fall. Why? Because as a principal of Kingdom living, God wanted all the offspring to leave behind their decision-making dependency with their families and create a new one with their spouse. Again, always operating with the principal of oneness—unity, agreement and togetherness. This means that the way that we were brought up and the decision processes we have learned (both healthy and unhealthy) are not to be predominant over each other. Rather, we need to forge a new way of processing with our spouse as together we seek God and God's will. This means that we're willing to open up our hearts to this new way with an objective of always seeking unity with both our spouse and God, which will bring us into the beauty of living in His kingdom. This calling is for every marriage to follow God's principal for every marriage—unity. It is to be first and foremost in all of our decision-making and processing through all the situations in our marriages. If we fully receive and believe that this is God's primary principle of life, we will readily embrace this truth and desire to learn to live in unity.

> **2 Chronicles 5: 11–14:**
> **11** *And it came to pass when the priests came out of the Most Holy Place (for all the priests who were present had sanctified themselves, without keeping to their divisions),* **12** *and the Levites who were the singers, all those of Asaph and Heman and Jeduthun, with their sons and their brethren, stood at the east end of the altar, clothed in white linen, having cymbals, stringed instruments and harps, and with them one hundred and twenty priests sounding with trumpets—* **13** *indeed it came to pass, when the trumpeters and singers were as one, to make one sound to be heard in praising and thanking the Lord, and when they lifted up their voice with the trumpets and cymbals and instruments of music, and praised the Lord, saying: "For He is good, For His mercy endures forever," that the house, the house of the Lord, was filled with a cloud,* **14** *so that the priests could not continue ministering because of the cloud; for the glory of the Lord filled the house of God.*

This is a wonderful story of unity. The priests gather together along with the singers and together begin praising and thanking God in worship. When their hearts became as one—in unity, in harmony, in agreement—the Shekinah glory filled the entire temple such that everyone had to stop since they were in such awe. The Shekinah glory is the overwhelming presence of God. It is experiencing the essence of God at such a deep spiritual level that it draws us truly into a heavenly place that can only be described as glorious, remarkable, exceptional, and amazing—true majesty and splendor. The principle here is that when we come together praising God, thanking God, seeking

God together and becoming one (unity), then his Shekinah glory will overwhelm us and bring us into such intimacy with Him that the ability to reach unity and understand unity will become easier and easier. We will be in awe at His solutions and direction for us that it will actually overwhelm us with amazement that our lives could ever be so blessed. The key here is to recognize that unity is brought about by our desire to pursue God. Unity with our spouse and with God. Then seek unity with God's work as He demonstrates His power and might. What a glorious privilege!

1 John 1: 7; 4: 7; 4: 12–19:

1: 7 But if we walk in the light as He is in the light, we have fellowship with one another, and the blood of Jesus Christ, His Son cleanses us from all sin.

4: 7 Beloved, let us love one another, for love is of God; and everyone who loves is born of God and knows God.

12 No one has seen God at any time. If we love one another, God abides in us, and His love has been perfected in us. 13 By this we know that we abide in Him, and He in us, because He has given us of His Spirit. 14 And we have seen and testify that the Father has sent the Son as Savior of the world. 15 Whoever confesses that Jesus is the Son of God, God abides in him, and he in God. 16 And we have known and believed the love that God has for us. God is love, and he who abides in love abides in God, and God in him. 17 Love has been perfected among us in this: that we may have boldness in the day of judgment; because as He is, so are we in this world. 18 There is no fear in love; but perfect love casts out fear, because fear involves torment. But he who fears has not been made perfect in love. 19 We love Him because He first loved us.

In 1 John we find an interesting commentary on oneness. First it tells us that if we walk together in the light, as God is in the light, (He is the light) we have fellowship with each other and are cleansed from sin (operating in the flesh, battling and opposing the work of the Spirit). Then he tells us that "love" is of God and as we love one another, we will demonstrate that we are of God and know God—have intimate relationship with God and are walking in the Spirit. We are to have affection toward one another as we seek each other's best interest through seeking God's will together. His wonderful will is known through reaching unity. He further tells us that love is experienced through abiding in Him—which means that we are walking in the Spirit, hearing and responding to His voice, enjoying His Rhema (Word of God) word to us and having a wonderful prayer dialogue in our relationship with Him. As a result of this experience and abiding, we are able to love one another and to assist each other in casting out fear—the root of much dissension and disagreement. In 1 John we learn that fear involves torment where we are overcome by a sense of foreboding that something negative is going to be an outcome of what we are deciding to do. Fear is the exact opposite of knowing that love will bring us to unity where we will experience the joy and the wonder of God's best and certainly not torment or oppression. As we are walking in Christ we will be receiving His love and fully able to give away His love to each other with a desire to bring each other along the spiritual path to the Kingdom and staying together in the center of God's Will. Our attitude shifts from trying to get our own way to seeking God's way and a surrendered heart that expresses love toward each other.

So, the concept of unity is actually borne of the very nature of God, which is love. This affection is a God-given gift that draws us together to give us the power of unity, where we will discover and live out God's will for our lives—His best and none better.

It is an interesting indicator that we are actually experiencing God's love. If we have a heart to seek and are experiencing unity, then it means that we are in the Spirit and receiving His love and thus able to freely give it away through unity.

Colossians 2: 2–3:

2 My purpose is that they may be encouraged in heart and united in love, so that they may have the full riches of complete understanding, in order that they may know the mystery of God, namely, Christ, 3 in whom are hidden all the treasures of wisdom and knowledge.

In Colossians, Paul states that by being knit together in love— walking in unity, united in affection for each other and for God, we will attain all the riches of the fullness of His understanding. We will have great knowledge of the work of God (experience fully His work not just know about His work) and we will receive the amazing treasures of wisdom and knowledge in our everyday lives. Instead of moving in the flesh toward disagreement and dissension, we will be moving closer and closer into the intimacy of God where we will receive amazing revelation and wisdom regarding the very circumstances we are trying to resolve. What a privilege this is that we can hear from God directly and what He has to say about the very issues we are struggling to resolve. This changes our hearts from maintaining our own position to seeking the wisdom and the Revelation that can only come from an all-knowing God. Wisdom from God is twofold: 1) what God proposes to do supernaturally in these circumstances; 2) what steps He wants us to take to bring about His grand will. It is important to note that wisdom is not just about how we can resolve things in the natural, but rather being directed by a supernatural God who can bring about His will through our actions. In unity, we find this wisdom. Why would we not desire to experience such an extraordinary gift as this!

Having caused our family to lose everything, due to my selfishness and refusing to process decisions with Linda, I was very sorrowful and discouraged. I felt very guilty at my poor decision-making, having lost all our money and the investor's money. I lived in guilt and could not let myself off the hook. I moped around and believe that I had caused us to be relegated to a mediocre life. I started to understand that being in the Word and talking to God through prayer was my only hope. So every day I would go walking and memorized the verses about forgiveness, particularly Romans 8:1: *"Therefore, there is now no condemnation in Christ Jesus."* Week after week I prayed this verse and knew that God had forgiven me (Linda had already forgiven me and only once said, "I told you so." For a long time, I could not forgive myself. Through prayer and abiding in this truth, it finally broke for me when I realized that since He had forgiven me, I had no right to stay in un-forgiveness toward myself. Finally, I was able to let myself off the hook through receiving the fullness of His forgiveness. At that time I began to hear God's voice as He asked me if I was willing to learn what it meant to go to unity with Linda. Having failed so miserably at not being in unity, I said absolutely yes. Through this process Linda and I learned all these principles of unity and how beautiful our life could be because of them. We only wish somebody had taught us earlier so that we might have avoided so many serious mistakes. Though I committed to going to unity, Linda was skeptical—and rightly so. My first commitment was to create a safe environment for her to share her true feelings, especially what she was feeling spiritually.

For the first several months, I made no comment on anything that she said. I only listened. She had to learn to trust me that I really cared and was willing to truly listen and process things together. As it became safe for her to share, she recognized that I was committed fully to the concept of making absolutely no decisions without unity. Soon, we began to experience God's restoration. Within three-years all we had lost financially was restored and we were experiencing extraordinary blessings in our marriage, in her family and in our work. I finally recognized that it wasn't critical for Linda to have logic behind her insights, only that she pay attention to her Spirit. If she felt uncomfortable, it just meant that we had to go deeper and further to pursue the truth of what God was revealing to us. We both recognized that it was important to go to neutrality on every decision (be willing to hear God's answer and not pursue our own) and stay in process until we reach unity in the Spirit. It was not negotiation or settling, but rather a deep unity of my spirit, Linda's spirit and the Holy Spirit. We knew that if we disagreed (which was necessary and an important part of the process) that either God would alter Linda's heart, alter my heart, or show us something brand-new that neither of us had considered. The decisions for choosing work, how to manage our money, how to raise the children, were all done in unity—and we began experiencing the wonder and awe of God's spectacular plan, restoring us fully. This is truly the good news—that no matter how many mistakes we've made or how deep a hole we dug, the Lord can restore it all. How beautiful is that?

CHAPTER 4
The Keys to Unity

Ephesians 4: 1–6:
1 I, therefore, the prisoner of the Lord, beseech you to walk
worthy of the calling with which you were called, 2 with
all lowliness and gentleness, with longsuffering, bearing
with one another in love, 3 endeavoring to keep the unity
of the Spirit in the bond of peace. 4 There is one body and
one Spirit, just as you were called in one hope of your call-
ing; 5 one Lord, one faith, one baptism; 6 one God and
Father of all, who is above all, and through all, and in
you all.

One of the primary keys to unity is a desire to go to unity.
Ephesians tells us that we are to walk worthy of our calling—
which is to walk with the Father in the Spirit, surrendering to
Him and seeking His will. This requires humility, gentleness,
patience and walking through the difficulties with each other
in love. We are called to work (attend to carefully) to keep the
unity of the Spirit in the "Bond of Peace—Shalom." Shalom is
a fabulous truth that does not mean just the absence of conflict, but rather favor, excellence, blessing, and joy. It is attained
through keeping the unity of the Spirit. Paul here gives us the
amazing reason why this is possible 100 percent of the time,
all the time—the same One Holy Spirit in me is also in my

41

spouse. Since it is one Spirit and He has one will, He cannot tell me something different than He is telling my spouse. Our decisions can always go to unity with the Spirit when we are willing to hear what the Spirit has to say about a particular issue or decision. If we have a heart to keep unity, knowing that unity can be reached 100 percent of the time, then we will get to unity. This is a key "criteria" for our ability to get to unity. If one of us doesn't really care to go to unity then the ability to get to unity is minimal and one person will tend to dominate. Linda and I have agreed that unless we get to unity we are not going to act or make any decisions independent of each other. However, if one of us actually didn't have the desire to go to unity, this approach would not be workable. One of us would control everything by just not agreeing and thus forcing the other to agree with us in order to proceed. By both of us knowing that the Spirit will get us to unity, and having a desire to go to unity, we get to unity. We are willing to let this take time and to allow our different viewpoints to be discussed through the process in a healthy way. A disagreement does not ruin our night or spoil our weekend. Instead, we just realize that we don't yet know God's will. We know He will show us His will because we are willing to pursue it with Him.

Equally important to our choice of not allowing dissension and discord to characterize our relationships, is that we together fully understand and desire to go to unity—because God will fulfill His role of getting us to unity 100 percent of the time, every time. Thus there is no reason to ever stay in strife, rather to just, in a healthy way, continue to pursue God's solution that will bring us to unity. Further this unity is not intellectual. It is not an analysis of information or a negotiated resolution. Rather, because it is unity of the Spirit, it is confirmed in our spirits. Thus, we have learned to trust this confirmation. If either one is uncomfortable or not at peace, even though not explainable through analysis, we still pay attention and realize that we are not in unity. The Spirit's role is to confirm this unity and uses our spirits to know when we are all in unity. Since it is a spiritual process, we must pay attention to the Spirit and not just to our natural intellect. In fact, the confirmation of the Spirit is way more significant than intellectual ability, because our intellectual ability is so limited compared to God. Unity is a commitment—and with that commitment means that we will together live in the best of God's life for us.

Philippians 2: 1–16:

1 Therefore if there is any consolation in Christ, if any comfort of love, if any fellowship of the Spirit, if any affection and mercy, 2 fulfill my joy by being like-minded, having the same love, being of one accord, of one mind. 3 Let nothing be done through selfish ambition or conceit, but in lowliness of mind let each esteem others better than himself. 4 Let each of you look out not only for his own interests, but also for the interests of others. 5 Let this mind be in you which was also in Christ Jesus, 6 who, being in the form of God, did not consider it robbery to be equal with God, 7 but made Himself of no reputation, taking the form of a bondservant, and coming in the likeness of men. 8 And being found in appearance as a man, He humbled Himself and became obedient to the point of death, even the death of the cross. 9 Therefore God also has highly exalted Him and given Him the name which is above every name, 10 that at the name of Jesus every knee should bow, of those in heaven, and of those on earth, and of those under the earth, 11 and that every tongue should confess that Jesus Christ is Lord, to the glory of God the Father. 12 Therefore, my beloved, as you have always obeyed, not as in my presence only, but now much more in my absence, work out your own salvation with fear and trembling; 13 for it is God who works in you both to will and to do for His good pleasure. 14 Do all things without complaining and disputing, 15 that you may become blameless and harmless, children of God without fault in the midst of a crooked and perverse generation, among whom you shine as lights in the world, 16 holding fast the word of life, so that I may rejoice in the day of Christ that I have not run in vain or labored in vain.

Another key is to fully understand and commit to "Our highest and best priority is to be like minded." Paul, here in Philippians, tells us that because we walk in Christ, in the fellowship of the Spirit and with each other, our highest priority is to be of one accord and one mind. These Greek words imply that we are to be united in spirit and at our deepest level to each other as we reach oneness and agreement on all issues. He further states that we have to be willing to relinquish self and in humility respect each other completely by honoring each other's opinions and viewpoints. Our priority is simple—go to UNITY.

Then he gives another key: work at differences in a healthy way. Paul makes an incredible statement that we are not only to look out for our own interest but for the interests of others. As we think of the simplicity of this truth, it does mean that we are to maintain our viewpoint and continue to express our viewpoint toward an issue or decision. There are three possibilities at this point when there are honest differences of opinion:

1. He shows me truth that changes my opinion and viewpoint.

2. He shows my spouse truth that changes her opinion and viewpoint.

3. He shows us both that neither of us had a complete view and needed a different perspective that neither of us understood.

We are to understand that: my heart is changed; my spouse's heart is changed; or God shows us something new. So it states that it is important to actually express your own interest—not to dominate or to selfishly manipulate but rather to express our own interest while we consider respectfully the interest of our spouse. This will open up our communications and give us joy just by talking things through as we listen and process until we see God's will.

The viewpoint must be truthful, at the heart level and not just acquiescence. It is actually important for us to create safe environments for our spouses to communicate, talk and share their views especially when they disagree with ours. This is important because that is how God will use the process to bring us to unity. A fundamental attitude must be established—we know we can get to unity and we want to. This speaks to me against resignation, compromise and against giving in to avoid the conflict. In most marriages and family relationships, there is typically a pattern where one person dominates. Everyone else sees conflict as disruptive and troublesome at a very deep level and thus it seems better to avoid the conflict at all cost rather than to experience it. The Word tells us that we are to process these differences in a healthy way and actually encourage each other to share and maintain their truth. God uses this method to bring us to His great will. Most of us will never understand that we settle for far less than God has planned. He uses this amazing process of working through differences of opinion to reveal His grand will and His beautiful solutions to our life circumstances. If we fully understood this, we would never again have a desire to force our opinion upon another, or to "win an argument." Rather, we would just accept that we do not yet know God's will, and to keep moving forward in our processing. It should never ruin our day, night or weekend. Even when we have reached an impasse, we do not let the emotion carry us to unhealthy places, Rather, let it go and know that we can come at it later, since God will reveal His truth and bring us to unity in the Spirit. Our primary role in marriage is to create a safe environment where there is freedom to express truth and together seek God's will. If it is healthy, then our dynamic is pleasant and no conflict can destroy that. We will deal specifically with how to process disagreements in Chapter 6.

> ### 2 Corinthians 13: 11–14:
> 11 *Finally, brethren, farewell. Become complete. Be of good comfort, be of one mind, live in peace; and the God of love and peace will be with you.* 12 *Greet one another with a holy kiss.* 13 *All the saints greet you.* 14 *The grace of the Lord Jesus Christ, and the love of God, and the communion of the Holy Spirit be with you all. Amen.*

Comfort each other by going to unity: Paul ends his letter to the Corinthians with an invitation to become complete (the fullness of salvation or wholeness in all aspects), be of good comfort to each other and become of one mind in peace—shalom. The Greek words used here for being of one mind is to gain understanding and wisdom—to think and feel in unity—reaching agreement on all issues. If our pursuit is unity, he says that the God of love and peace (the fullness of God's favor, security, safety, prosperity) will be with us. In other words, as we pursue unity, God promises a unity that will lead us into the joy of love and shalom. Our lives will have God's favor and we will experience awe and wonder as we enjoy every aspect of our lives.

In order to reach unity, we are called to walk with God:

> ### Ephesians 5: 1–4; 6–11; 15 –21:
> 1 *Therefore be imitators of God as dear children.* 2 *And walk in love, as Christ also has loved us and given Himself for us, an offering and a sacrifice to God for a*

*sweet-smelling aroma. **3** But fornication and all uncleanness or covetousness, let it not even be named among you, as
is fitting for saints; **4** neither filthiness, nor foolish talking,
nor coarse jesting, which are not fitting, but rather giving
of thanks…**6** Let no one deceive you with empty words,
for because of these things the wrath of God comes upon
the sons of disobedience. **7** Therefore do not be partakers
with them. **8** For you were once darkness, but now you are
light in the Lord. Walk as children of light **9** (for the fruit
of the Spirit is in all goodness, righteousness, and truth),
10 finding out what is acceptable to the Lord. **11** And have
no fellowship with the unfruitful works of darkness, but
rather expose them….**15** See then that you walk circum-
spectly, not as fools but as wise, **16** redeeming the time,
because the days are evil. **17** Therefore do not be unwise,
but understand what the will of the Lord is. **18** And do not
be drunk with wine, in which is dissipation; but be filled
with the Spirit, **19** speaking to one another in psalms and
hymns and spiritual songs, singing and making melody in
your heart to the Lord, **20** giving thanks always for all
things to God the Father in the name of our Lord Jesus
Christ, **21** submitting to one another in the fear of God.*

Ephesians 5 tells us that we are to walk with God in a certain
way:

1. Walk in love—with affection for God and for others.

2. Walk in the light—always pursue truth.

3. Walk in wisdom—seek God's revelation and insight.

Walk means to make the way, progress, make due use of
opportunity. **We walk in love (affection, good will, benevo-
lence, feasting)** by receiving the love that Christ has given us

which is grace and mercy when we don't deserve it. He gave himself for us as an offering to God so that we could have intimacy with God himself. He says that walking in the flesh, which results in the list that we described previously such as fornication, uncleanness, covetousness, filthiness, foolish talking, and coarse jesting, takes us away from walking in love and further not being able to inherit the kingdom of Christ and God. This does not mean that we will not go to heaven, which is eternally secure for us if we truly have received Christ as our Lord and Savior, but rather that we will not experience the benefits of the Kingdom of God as we are walking in love. We will actually walk outside the Kingdom of God and experience the consequences of walking in our own counsel. It says that the wrath of God will come on us so that we are not receiving the wonder and the blessedness of God's life. Rather, we are walking further and further away with the consequences becoming more and more severe. He tells us important truths about this process:

1. Be thankful and not complaining or grumbling looking for the negative, but rather praising God for all that He has given us and that we are His children—recipients of his love.

2. Do not partake with people who are walking in the flesh and bringing you onto their path. Rather we are to stay walking in love and invite them to our path, walking with God. This love then gets expressed to each other because we care for one another, want the best for each other, and continue to assist each other in walking in God's love as we are thankful and recognizing that He has given himself for us and wants our best.

John 3: 19–21:

19 And this is the condemnation, that the light has come into the world, and men loved darkness rather than light, because their deeds were evil. 20 For everyone practicing evil hates the light and does not come to the light, lest his deeds should be exposed. 21 But he who does the truth comes to the light, that his deeds may be clearly seen, that they have been done in God."

"Walking in the light" means we will experience the Spirit's goodness, righteousness and truth. Goodness means that we will receive the best and none better, be covered and enjoying the righteousness of Christ who has given himself for us, is completely holy and we will begin to open our hearts to truth in all aspects.

John tells us that everyone who hates the light and does not come to the light is actually practicing evil. Those who come to the truth and desire the truth will be living in the light and the beauty of God. This has very interesting implications. If we are unwilling to let the light expose everything about our circumstances, our situations, our feelings, our heart etc. we actually are practicing evil. Evil is defined as not of God, leading to frustration, difficulty, pain, hardness and oppression. To remedy this is to come to the light exposing our inner-most feelings willingly. This means that in whatever situation we are facing, we are willing to let all truth be known. In a marriage, this means that we openly share what we know with each other completely and let the truth be known without manipulation or reservation. We are always interested in receiving more data, more facts, more information—particularly discernment about what may be operating spiritually in our circumstances and situations. The more truth that we know and receive, the easier it will be to go to unity. As we walk in the light, John tells us specifically to find out what is acceptable to God. In other words to discover, learn and receive what is God's will and truth about our decision, issue or situation. If we are willing to communicate truth to each other, then we do not become defensive nor try to cover up things that may not support our position, but rather expose it all openly. Coming to the light means completely transparent communications and never being afraid to share everything including my thinking and my deepest feelings. If we are willing to process the truth, it will be known and we will find out what is acceptable to God.

As we are walking in wisdom, John tells us to not be foolish (by trying to figure things out on our own—by practicing evil) but rather to understand completely what is the will of God. His role is to clarify His will and to give us great discernment, revelation and understanding about His will and the reason for His will. With this understanding will come the wisdom to see that God is asking us to walk into His will. With great wisdom (the word wisdom here refers to the practical things of life and how to operate in a way that benefits us and reflects the very nature of God) we can give testimony to the nature of God in us. He states that the key to this is to be filled to overflowing with the Spirit and continue to speak to each other from his Word with thanksgiving and making melody and harmony in our hearts together. This is a heart attitude and a heart issue. As we desire to make melody and harmony together we will acquire wisdom and will find out the will of God. This wisdom will allow us to understand that two people in agreement will be on His path to enjoy and receive all the benefits He has available to us. He ends the section with an amazing statement: submit to one another. This mitigates the artificial hierarchy that is often established, where the wife is supposed to submit to her husband. Obviously, he is not talking about submitting to her husband in decision-making because he just explained that the way to reach decisions is to: walk in love, walk in the light, and walk in wisdom (finding out what is acceptable to the Lord and understanding His will). That requires a mutual submission and a respectful submission to the process until you get to unity. Ephesians goes on to state that a wife is to surrender or submit to her husband as her husband submits to Christ—meaning to the process of reaching unity and not selfishly going on their own path. The corollary to this is for the husband to love his wife as Christ loves the church, which is to help them walk in love, walk in the light, and walk in wisdom. The most amazing thing about this is that God's will is best and none better, so why would we not want to walk in love, in the light and in wisdom together to achieve and receive the Best?

> *Galatians 5: 16; 22–25:*
> *22 But the fruit of the Spirit is love, joy, peace, patience, kindness, goodness, faithfulness, 23 gentleness and self-control. Against such things there is no law. 24 Those who belong to Christ Jesus have crucified the sinful nature with its passions and desires. 25 Since we live by the Spirit, let us keep in step with the Spirit.*

A big key to unity is very simple—walking in the Spirit (keeping in step) and not in the flesh. This means that we will be willing to surrender our will to the Spirit, go where He directs without reservation. By following Him, the fruits of the Spirit: love, joy, peace, patience, kindness, goodness, gentleness and self-control become our nature. These characteristics give us the ability to enjoy each other and respectfully handle disagreements on our march toward unity. If we walk in the Spirit by following the Spirit, by definition, we will not be walking in the flesh seeking our own way. Pursuing unity actually keeps us walking in the Spirit because we are working to find out what is acceptable to God and to understand His will. As we understand His will better, we then find it easier to walk in His will and stay in the Spirit and not stray to the flesh.

Romans 8: 5; 12–17:

5 For those who live according to the flesh set their minds on the things of the flesh, but those who live according to the Spirit, the things of the Spirit.

12 Therefore, brethren, we are debtors—not to the flesh, to live according to the flesh. 13 For if you live according to the flesh you will die; but if by the Spirit you put to death the deeds of the body, you will live. 14 For as many as are led by the Spirit of God, these are sons of God. 15 For you did not receive the spirit of bondage again to fear, but you received the Spirit of adoption by whom we cry out, "Abba, Father." 16 The Spirit Himself bears witness with our spirit that we are children of God, 17 and if children, then heirs—heirs of God and joint heirs with Christ, if indeed we suffer with Him, that we may also be glorified together.

Paul further defines what it means to walk in the Spirit; First, he tells us to set our minds on the things of the Spirit. In order to set our minds on the things of the Spirit, we must be abiding in His Word - the expression of His Truth and Will for each of us. Furthermore, we do gain insight into many of the things that are on His heart:

1. **Genesis 12:1–3: the Covenant**. He desires to bless us and to make us a blessing. (We are to receive the goodness of God and His life for us with a call to give it away.)

2. **Isaiah 61: 1–4: we are to be anointed by the Holy Spirit to preach the good news.** The good news is that He desires to:

   a. Heal the brokenhearted.

   b. Proclaim liberty to the captives.

c. Open up the prison to those who are bound up.

d. Proclaim the acceptable year of the Lord and to know that those who oppose us will receive God's vengeance.

e. To comfort and console those who are mourning.

f. To give beauty for ashes (restore the very things in life that we or others have ruined and are currently worthless).

g. Provide joy and praise for heaviness.

h. Rebuild and restore what has been ruined in our life.

3. **Jeremiah 29: 11–14: to know and experience the fantastic plans that God has made for us.**—He only has plans for our hope in a wonderful future; No plans to harm or oppress us. His will is best and none better and thus, as we experience these plans, which are His will, we will be experiencing the beauty of the blessings of a life of God.

4. **Acts 1: 5–8: we are to be His witnesses.** We reflect His life and glory for us to those around us. We invite them to see the beauty of walking with God and the benefits of walking with God. As they do, they will have a desire to learn what we have learned and thus seek God themselves.

We could go on and on, but you get the idea. The truths of Scripture are valid and are what's on the heart and mind of the Spirit. In order for us to walk in the Spirit we are to set our mind on these things and not be trying to establish our own agenda or figure things out on our own. Paul further explains that we are no longer obligated to live a life of the flesh which leads us to failure or mediocrity (which the church has promoted as being normal), but rather to live a life of the Spirit where we are being led by the Spirit. This means that we desire to be led (be guided into new places in our life), hear His voice, receive clarity regarding His will, follow His steps of obedience, and submit all of our decisions to the Spirit. This is the beauty of unity. We have a built in "checker" with our spouse. Together, we will know the will of God and be led by the Spirit as we reach unity because we both will confirm that we understand the will of God and know what steps to take.

Paul tells us that we need not live in the bondage of fear but rather in the Spirit of "Abba, Father"—which means that we are toddlers completely enjoying the life of God. The wonderful thing about toddlers is that they do not fret or fear about anything. They are not worried about their career or their finances or the impact of the world upon them. Rather, their question is rather simple: "what do we get to do today, daddy? "Because they have a heart to follow, they are willing to do anything that the parents say. If I say to my grandsons that we are going to go to the movie, they say okay. If I say were going to go outside and play ball, they say okay. If I say we are going to the store, they say okay. What toddlers care about is just being with us. They don't evaluate whether the things that we asked them to be a part of are good or bad. They know intuitively that being with us is nothing but joy and fun. That is the heart of being led by the Spirit, we are to be toddlers. Not determining on our own that what the father is asking us to do or be, whether it is good or not, but rather, to just say yes and enjoy the walk. Furthermore the Spirit's role is to confirm with us that we are children of God and thus to receive all the benefits of the children of God—a child of the King. We have a wonderful recent example in the marriage of Kate Middleton to Prince William. Kate was considered a commoner with none of the privileges of being a child of the English Kingdom. When she married into the royal family, she became a royal with all of the privileges of being royalty. She now has access to the income of the royalty, to the palaces of the royalty, to the staff of the royalty, etc. because she has been confirmed now as a child of the king and queen. She has not rejected this but rather embraced it. God wants us to experience the same thing. We are children of the King and will experience the wonderful benefits of being children of the King. The Spirit's role is to confirm that we are children of the King. Being led by the Spirit shows us how beautiful it is to live the life of the Kingdom.

Colossians 3: 12–17:
12 Therefore, as the elect of God, holy and beloved, put on tender mercies, kindness, humility, meekness, longsuffering; 13 bearing with one another, and forgiving one another, if anyone has a complaint against another; even as Christ forgave you, so you also must do. 14 But above all these things put on love, which is the bond of perfection. 15 And let the peace of God rule in your hearts, to which also you were called in one body; and be thankful. 16 Let the word of Christ dwell in you richly in all wisdom, teaching and admonishing one another in psalms and hymns and spiritual songs, singing with grace in your hearts to the Lord. 17 And whatever you do in word or deed, do all in the name of the Lord Jesus, giving thanks to God the Father through Him.

Let Peace be the determining factor in reaching Unity:

Colossians tells us to let peace rule our life. This word "rule" means to umpire. An umpire is able to make clear calls—safe/out, in/foul, strike/ball, first down/not first down, etc. So, we are to let the aspect of peace, which means harmony and agreement, serve to determine if we have reached unity or not. Peace is based on our peace in the Spirit and not based on logic or manufactured feelings. Thus as we are processing decisions and issues of our marriage or relationships, we are to pursue discussions and processing further until we both, or all, have peace in our hearts about this particular decision or issue. Practically, we allow our spouse or friend to share their true understanding of peace or lack of peace in the process. The requirement is for both or all parties to have a heart to seek God's will and go to peace with the Spirit. As discussed previously, if we are operating in the flesh and thus self-centered, this aspect of letting peace umpire our life will not be valid—since the Spirit is not causing any lack of peace but rather our self. If each person desires to know God's will and surrender to his will through unity with the Spirit and with each other, then Spirit's using of peace as our umpire will be simple to follow. If we have peace and unity (agreement) then we can have great confidence that we are understanding and cleared to move forward in our agreement. If we do not have peace and unity, then we are not to take action, but rather to continue to seek truth and process together until we reach unity.

As we lived in unity, we can bear witness to how spectacular our life has been ever since. We followed these very simple principles:

1. We can get to unity on every decision, 100 percent of the time, all the time. The Holy Spirit is resident in both Linda and me and will speak His will to us. He cannot speak different things.

2. It is okay to disagree. In fact, it is important for each of us to hold integrity with our true thoughts, beliefs and insights. It does not ruin our night or week or weekend. We just believe that we don't yet know God's will but we will.

3. We both are called to walk in the Spirit, constantly go to neutrality, and stay in process until we get to unity.

4. We get to unity by both seeking God's will.

5. We set our minds on things above and do not let the logic of the world dictate our decisions.

6. We let peace "umpire" our decisions. We don't negotiate and we don't compromise. Instead, we work through the issue until we both feel at peace in the Spirit and know that this decision or action is God's will.

After being restored, we've experienced wonderful success in a variety of business endeavors. We made sure to stay in balance with each other and our life together in God; God used us to start a new church in Boulder—Flatirons Community Church. It is now the largest church in Colorado. (At a certain point in its early growth we were faced with either going full-time or finding a full-time pastor. The Lord spoke to both of us that it was time to move on. We recruited a full-time pastor who helped lead the church to over 5,000 members. Now a second pastor is to lead it to 20,000 members. We were in complete unity on that decision and have seen the result of God's will.) Next, God asked us to step in as senior pastor in a troubled church—Park Community Church in Chicago. (The church has been restored and is currently one of the largest and most vibrant churches in the city.) Because of its success, many urged me to look for greater opportunities to help troubled churches. Linda and I have learned to never just proceed along a logical path, but rather to seek God on all things. He spoke to us that we were done with that activity and to return to Colorado and enjoy our marriage and disciple our children, which we did. Shortly thereafter, we were led to more fully develop a retreat ministry which had begun while we were pastors in Chicago.

Today this ministry is thriving as we teach believers to abide in the Vine, hear from God, and learn to go to unity with spouses or Godly friends. We have 16 Leader couples in the ministry who are conducting retreats all over the country. Because of them, many other people are experiencing the joy of abiding and the grand life that comes through unity.

A few examples will illustrate how going to unity works. In the beginning of a particular year, during my prayer time as I was asking the Father about important things for the particular year, He spoke to me that we were to sell our Chicago condo. When we served as pastors in Chicago, we purchased this phenomenal place—southeast corner on the thirty-third-floor overlooking the lake and downtown Chicago. Every Wednesday and Saturday in the summer we had the privilege of "front row seats" to remarkable firework shows. We had purchased the unit from an estate and completely remodeled it, with floor-to-ceiling windows. Linda and I fully enjoyed its beauty (but we still maintained a home in Colorado). We had built special memories there with our children and grandchildren who often came to visit. While the condo was truly spectacular in all regards, being asked to sell it was pretty easy for me. When I spoke to Linda about what God had spoken, she reacted negatively and said she did not feel good about that. In the past I would have argued and debated her until she agreed. Now having learned that the value and truth of unity, I just ask her to go to God herself and seek His will. I had to say nothing as I knew that we would get to the same place if we both have a heart to go. For the first couple weeks, Linda recognized that she was not at neutrality. The condo held such great memories. She hoped to create more in the future. So she first had to process with God as to why she was not neutral and then ask God to help her get to neutral. Every day she would consider her response regarding the possibility of the answer changing to "sell it." Finally, she did come to the place of neutrality and was open to God's answer. He spoke to her that yes, we were to sell the condo. Having heard from God and confirmed in her spirit that it was a "yes" and I had also heard a "yes" from God (during this time, I too was seeking God's answer and confirmation so had to go to neutrality as well), we were in unity with the Spirit and knew the answer. We put up the condo in April and sold it in the middle of July—2008; just over the peak of the market and right before the crash in the fall. Had we not listened to God, it is likely that we still would have owned that condo and lost most of the equity that we gained when we sold it.

With these funds in hand, we had an opportunity to do a 1031 exchange, whereby we take the funds and invest in a new like property without having to pay any taxes on the gain. As I was pondering the next investment, I had the brilliant idea to purchase an office building in Castle Rock and move our company into it, as well as leasing to other businesses. I went to Linda and expressed my new idea. She said that her spirit did not feel right about this, as this was the cause of our previous bankruptcy and that we had committed to never going down that path again. I recognized immediately that her spirit was right and we should not pursue that idea at all. (Remember, this was the summer of 2008, and had I acted as I normally did in the past, we would've had another disaster on our hands).

So while I was praying about where to make the investment, if at all, I heard on the radio about foreclosures. I went to Linda and shared this possibility and she said that she felt much better about pursuing that, so we did. With a 1031, there is a time limit. If we you miss the deadline, taxes would have to be paid. Though we were under a time limit constraint, we never let it dictate our decisions. If we missed the deadline, then we would know that it was God's will to not invest in another property but rather to just pay the taxes and keep the money in the bank. We were in neutrality, and it made no difference to us. We never let time pressure push us to get ahead of God's will. If we were not in unity, we would let the deadline pass. In this case, Linda was able to find a foreclosure that worked and we were able to purchase a house significantly below market (though later in 2008 and 2009, it was at the new market price because of the drop in the economy. We did not lose any equity through the downturn. Several years later, we were led to sell this one and invest in another foreclosure. Through an up-and-down market, we have been given step by step instruction regarding each decision. We did this in unity and know that God's will is best and none better. Why would we not?

CHAPTER 5

Unity Comes Through Abiding in the Word

Nehemiah 8:1–12:

1 Now all the people gathered together as one man in the open square that was in front of the Water Gate; and they told Ezra the scribe to bring the Book of the Law of Moses, which the Lord had commanded Israel. 2 So Ezra the priest brought the Law before the assembly of men and women and all who could hear with understanding on the first day of the seventh month. 3 Then he read from it in the open square that was in front of the Water Gate from morning until midday, before the men and women and those who could understand; and the ears of all the people were attentive to the Book of the Law. 4 So Ezra the scribe stood on a platform of wood which they had made for the purpose; and beside him, at his right hand, stood Mattithiah, Shema, Anaiah, Urijah, Hilkiah, and Maaseiah; and at his left hand Pedaiah, Mishael, Malchijah, Hashum, Hashbaddanah, Zechariah, and Meshullam. 5 And Ezra opened the book in the sight of all the people, for he was standing above all the people; and when he opened it, all the people stood up. 6 And Ezra blessed the Lord, the great God. Then all the people answered, "Amen, Amen!"

*while lifting up their hands. And they bowed their heads
and worshiped the Lord with their faces to the ground. 7
Also Jeshua, Bani, Sherebiah, Jamin, Akkub, Shabbethai,
Hodijah, Maaseiah, Kelita, Azariah, Jozabad, Hanan,
Pelaiah, and the Levites, helped the people to understand
the Law; and the people stood in their place. 8 So they
read distinctly from the book, in the Law of God; and they
gave the sense, and helped them to understand the reading.
9 And Nehemiah, who was the governor, Ezra the priest
and scribe, and the Levites who taught the people said to
all the people, "This day is holy to the Lord your God; do
not mourn nor weep." For all the people wept, when they
heard the words of the Law. 10 Then he said to them, "Go
your way, eat the fat, drink the sweet, and send portions
to those for whom nothing is prepared; for this day is holy
to our Lord. Do not sorrow, for the joy of the Lord is your
strength." 11 So the Levites quieted all the people, saying,
"Be still, for the day is holy; do not be grieved." 12 And all
the people went their way to eat and drink, to send portions and rejoice greatly, because they understood the words
that were declared to them.*

After Nehemiah had completed the wall in Jerusalem and
began restoring the protection and the economy of Israel. He
understood that the people had not yet received the fullness of
God's will for Israel. So, he brought out the book of the Law
(Scripture—God's Word) and had Ezra the priest read it aloud
to all (men, women and children) who had gathered with a
heart to hear truth and be attentive to what God was saying. As
Ezra read, the other priests gathered with the people in small
groups, further explaining and helping everyone understand
what God was speaking. So the process is very straight forward
and still valid for us today:

1. Be committed to regular time with Christ in the Spirit through abiding in His Word:

Luke 10: 38—42:
38 Now it happened as they went that He entered a certain village; and a certain woman named Martha welcomed Him into her house. 39 And she had a sister called Mary, who also sat at Jesus' feet and heard His word. 40 But Martha was distracted with much serving, and she approached Him and said, "Lord, do You not care that my sister has left me to serve alone? Therefore tell her to help me." 41 And Jesus answered and said to her, "Martha, Martha, you are worried and troubled about many things. 42 But one thing is needed, and Mary has chosen that good part, which will not be taken away from her."

We are not to be thinking that our Christian life is all about working for Christ, even to do good Christian things, but rather our highest and best priority is to sit at His feet, abiding. The Words that Christ used here imply that Martha, in her desire to serve Him, was actually serving herself—to appear that she was more righteous than Mary and receive approval through her work (the basis of her self esteem). Thus, the focus on tasks (even serving tasks) was creating distraction and a troubling heart. Instead of being able to receive God's revelation and wisdom, she was worried about her own stuff and equating serving with God's goodness. Mary "CHOSE" (made a conscious choice, not an automatic one) to be abiding with Christ—doing what He called good: *being pleasant, agreeable, joyful, happy, excellent, distinguished, upright, honorable.* When in dialogue in a Jewish home of that time, neither would be standing or sitting in a chair, but rather reclining next to each other. Mary's sitting at His feet was not listening to a sermon or theological concepts, but a back and forth dialogue with Christ speaking truth that meant something in Mary's life. Mary would be asking questions and making statements, with Christ answering and asking her questions. This is a wonderful picture of abiding—not to be troubled and distracted with our daily tasks (even good tasks), but to always choose the good thing—spending time in dialogue with Christ.

2. Read the Word where God is speaking to us:

Psalms 119: 16 and 17: "*I will delight in your statutes; I will not forget your Word. Deal bountifully with your servant, that I may live and keep your Word.*"

Psalms 119: 57: "*The Lord is my portion; I promise to keep your Words.*"

Our delight and our commitment are to be regularly (daily) reading His Word. Be willing to hear from Him—delighting in His Word and committing to receiving and carrying out what He reveals to us.

Proverbs 4: 1–7; 20–23:
1 Hear, my children, the instruction of a father, And give attention to know understanding; 2 For I give you good doctrine: Do not forsake my law. 3 When I was my father's son, Tender and the only one in the sight of my mother, 4 He also taught me, and said to me: "Let your heart retain my words; Keep my commands, and live. 5 Get wisdom! Get understanding! Do not forget, nor turn away from the words of my mouth. 6 Do not forsake her, and she will preserve you; Love her, and she will keep you. 7 Wisdom is the principal thing; Therefore get

wisdom. And in all your getting, get understanding...20
My son, give attention to my words; Incline your ear to
my sayings. **21** *Do not let them depart from your eyes;*
Keep them in the midst of your heart; **22** *For they are life*
to those who find them, And health to all their flesh. **23**
Keep your heart with all diligence, For out of it spring
the issues of life.

3. What is necessary for the Word to become real and powerful in our lives? Practically, how does this work?

The key is to pay attention to what the Lord is saying to us—not just "doing a devotion" or our own idea of Bible study. Rather, we should be listening and processing what He is speaking and has on His heart to reveal to us. This will be where we are paying the closest attention, where there is a recurring word or idea shown to us over and over (we might hear it at church, see it on TV, in a book, etc.). We will have a strong desire to pursue it further because it is stimulating our heart. We are called to stay with it (pay attention) until the Words and the truth of the living Words fill our hearts and souls. We will understand them, receive them, process them, and then totally believe them. Then we can pray the promise of these Words with complete expectation that they will come to pass (AMEN) in our real lives—both in circumstances and in the transformation of our hearts that lead us to freedom.

Jeremiah. 15 and 16
16 *Your words were found, and I ate them, And Your word*
was to me the joy and rejoicing of my heart; For I am
called by Your name, O Lord God of hosts.

We have to "eat" His Words—a sheep ruminates on the grass she eats—chews and chews, swallows, digests some, moves it back up into her mouth to continue chewing, swallowing, and digesting until the grass has become meat, a part the sheep. We are to ruminate in the same way. Chew on the Word, ruminate on it (ponder, consider, process), swallow it (receive and take it into your heart) and digest it (believe it so deeply that it becomes part of us and our life). We do this by journaling the truth of these verses, going deeper into the Greek and Hebrew (use easy software programs such as *Crosswalk.com* or *studylight. org*), journaling our thoughts and questions about the verses, journaling what we are hearing and the insights we are receiving from the Spirit. AND, do all this with pure joy and rejoicing! Even when being convicted. So it is meant to stimulate us and take us into His promises, His truth and His life. If we are not receiving the Words in joy (which brings stimulation, fullness, celebration), then either we are studying the Word with our intellect and only seeing it as rules, or not studying where He wants us in the Word.

Luke 2: 41–52:

42 And when He was twelve years old, they went up to Jerusalem according to the custom of the feast. 43 When they had finished the days, as they returned, the Boy Jesus lingered behind in Jerusalem. And Joseph and His mother did not know it; 44 but supposing Him to have been in the company, they went a day's journey, and sought Him among their relatives and acquaintances. 45 So when they did not find Him, they returned to Jerusalem, seeking Him. 46 Now so it was that after three days they found Him in the temple, sitting in the midst of the teachers, both listening to them and asking them questions. 47 And all who heard Him were astonished at His understanding and answers. 48 So when they saw Him, they were amazed; and His mother said to Him, "Son, why have You done this to us? Look, Your father and I have sought You anxiously." 49 And He said to them, "Why did you seek Me? Did you not know that I must be about My Father's business?" 50 But they did not understand the statement which He spoke to them.

We are to approach the Word as the boy Christ approached learning—by listening, asking questions, stating what He understood and giving answers to the questions being asked by His teachers. Our time in the Word should mimic His. We carry it out through our journaling of our time in the Word when He is speaking to us. Our journaling every day is not just a diary. Rather, it is responding to the Words from Scripture that He speaks to us—listening, asking questions, and writing what we understand. Our journal should contain: what are we hearing from God? What questions does this bring to mind regarding ways I might learn this? How will I accomplish it? What does it mean? What am I to understand? Then document what you understand at this moment. At least once a week, write in your journal what you understand from that week's time of abiding—without looking at that week's journal entries—this shows you what you have received into your hearts this week. Then, go back over your week's journal entries to see what you have missed or not fully received or understood. Reviewing sets up where to concentrate next week until Christ's message is fully received. Make this is a true joy, never seeing it as a "what is wrong with me" question. The Spirit continually encourages us to stay abiding until the Word is received, believed and you are able to live it out. Listen, question, summarize—do exactly what Christ did to demonstrate the process to us.

Here are specific processes to understand how truly to "Abide in the Spirit, in the Word." Begin practicing these:

ABIDING IN THE WORD

1. Pursue your interest. What interesting Word or thought the Spirit been piquing your interest with? What do you already know God is laying on your heart?

2. Write out the specific Scriptures—Find a good Cross Reference Study Bible with helps and concordance. NASB; NEV; NKJV (Spirit Filled Life Bible is particularly good as it includes translations of Greek and Hebrew words); Amplified—note: do not use paraphrase as primary Bible, only for some additional help. You can also go to *www.biblegateway.com* or *www.crosswalk.com* for different translations. Spend some time understanding the context of the specific Bible Book from which the verse is taken. Also, do not read just the specific verse, but read the entire paragraph for context.

3. Cross reference specific verses by using your Cross Reference Study Bible, which will take you to other truths about that particular revelation. Use the concordance at the back of your Bible to facilitate your Word studies or go to: *www.biblegateway.com* or *www.crosswalk.com*. As you spend time in the cross-referenced or word study verses, let the "quickening" of the Spirit lead you. Only when you are sure He is speaking to you should you spend time further processing. If a verse doesn't strike your heart much, don't spend any further time on it. Instead, continue to cross-reference other verses that strike your heart or go to another verse from your Word study.

4. Write out your thoughts about:

   a. What this says about the character of God?

   b. What God has done, is doing or promises to do?

   c. Are there any conditions to what God promises? (If...then)

   d. What are my responsibilities or responses?

5. Go deeper into the Hebrew and Greek meaning of the Words He is speaking to you: (*www.crosswalk.com*,) go under the heading "Bible Search on right" and click underneath this on "*Powered by BibleStudyTools.com*"; then on the next screen click on "Read" in the heading sections in black at the top of site; and then on "Interlinear Bible"—on that screen, type in word or verses: when the verses come up along with the Greek and Hebrew on the next screen, click on your chosen word, then from the next screen, print the Hebrew or Greek word meanings.

6. Memorize the verses (word for word). Write the verses on 3x5 index cards to help you remember.

7. Journal your thoughts:

   a. Do I believe this in my heart (is it settled?) Why or why not?

   b. (What do I struggle with and what experiences in my life, work against what I am receiving in the Word?)

   c. How do these words apply to my situation and me today?

    d.   How is God calling me to adjust my life to Him and His will?

    e.   What thoughts come to me about all this?

    f.   Dialogue with the Father your thoughts. Ask for clarity, understanding, wisdom and faith.

8. Pray the promises: Ask God to fulfill what He has said to you.

9. Commit time with a friend or spouse, sharing your journal—what God is saying directly to you.

    a.   Discuss feelings, reactions, & insights—why is this verse particularly important to me.

    b.   Study specific verses that you share with each other.

    c.   Pray verses together.

The key to abiding is to be authentic as you dialogue with the Father through the Spirit. You process the truth of His Words by journaling—the meaning of the actual words, your thoughts about these words, and how they apply to your life now. It is important to spend time every day in abiding. Don't relegate this to once a week or less. Thus twenty to thirty minutes a day is much more valuable than one or two hours, once a week. If each person is abiding, then there will be much to share and process together as spouses and mates; or as singles with Spirit led friends.

Coming to unity is not a matter of working through facts and logic. Rather it is coming to unity and oneness with the Holy Spirit. This requires abiding. Linda and I each have our personal walk with God. We "camp out" in Scripture where He is speaking personally to us (Rhema). We follow the above process through receiving the life of the Word, journaling our understanding, questions, our understanding, our revelation; and through going deeper through cross-referencing and word studies. At least once a week, we meet together and share our journals to discuss what we have been hearing from the Father, in Christ, through the Spirit. I listen to Linda share and ask questions as we read the Scriptures together. I sometimes notice things that she might not have seen that we can discuss at a deeper level. Then after she is assured, I will share and she will ask questions. It is difficult to describe, but the very revelations that we are personally receiving are a great help as we go to unity. Further, we are open to hearing the Lord speaking or reveal other verses in the truths that have impact on our decisions. At the end of our time together we pray for each other, asking the Father to fulfill what He has spoken and to lift up each other with any struggles and/or doubts that they are experiencing. This serves two big purposes: 1) It shows that we care and desire to be each other's best cheerleader and encourager. 2) We are an intercessor for them. Because we have spent this time, we know that during the days ahead we are always praying for each other.

For example, when we were at a phase in fast-growing Living Waters Retreat Ministry, Linda and I were leading all the retreats. We knew that our capacity was at its max. We didn't know how to minister to any more souls. Linda was led to Exodus 18:18 where Moses was faced with a similar issue. His father-in-law, Jethro, came and spoke,

"The thing that you do is not good, you will wear yourself out, you are not able to perform it by yourself; listen now to my voice; I will give you counsel, and God will be with you: you shall select from all the people able men and women such as fear God, full of truth, hating covetousness and placing such over them to be rulers of others."

This was our answer. We were not to continue to do all the retreats ourselves, but rather to build leaders who could continue the great work. Our task now would be to develop material, train our successors, and facilitate their retreat leadership. Through our abiding, we received God's Word, and in unity understood God's will. It has turned out to be a most beautiful thing—we now have sixteen couples leading retreats around the country.

In our retreats, we could share example after example of how abiding has led to unity. We have seen scores of couples in troubled marriages come to joy and splendor. In many cases, because they had come to the end of their emotional ability to live as husband and wife, the couples were considering separating. Through learning to abide and go to unity, they began receiving God's word about themselves and then about their marriages and how to look to Him to bring unity to their decisions. In each case, they have gone from conflict and emotional separation, to amazing and supernatural works of God—including overcoming bankruptcy, problems with children, finances, etc. Everyone at our retreats learns that without abiding, unity is simply a more proficient way of negotiating. Most importantly, they learn that abiding leads them into an intimate relationship with the Spirit and the ability to process things together, in humility, seeking God's will, until they reach unity. The results are beyond description and all we can say is why would anyone not?

In another situation, a couple that attended one of our European retreats had an unusual experience. The husband was overwhelmed by all the activities in which he was involved. His wife was suffering because, instead of being first in his life, she was at the end of the line. We helped them see how abiding in the Vine was critical to their future and that as branches, we all need to be occasionally pruned. This means cutting back on our activities, even though we believe them to be growing in order to be fruitful for God and for ourselves. The couple agreed to prioritize all their activities, including all the ministries that they were involved in and to work at cutting back until they could put each other as a priority and have margin in their life. We helped them learn what it meant to abide personally and then as a couple. Through that abiding, they gained the strength to cut back their activities and make decisions in unity going forward. They have come to a spectacular place of living together in the Spirit and experiencing the grandeur of God's blessed life for them. Watching their joy grow has truly been remarkable and they have continued for over ten years now in this abiding process. They bear witness to its beauty.

CHAPTER 6

How to Handle Disagreements and Differences of Opinion

As we are normally operating in the flesh, we view disagreements and differences of opinion as problematic. Our typical goal is to win every debate or argument - persuading the other party that we are right and work to manipulate information and response in our favor. As we now understand the significance and beauty of unity in the Spirit, we need to see disagreements and differences in a new light—actually, they are a necessary and significant part of the process to come to unity.

Acts 15: 1–6:

1 And certain men came down from Judea and taught the brethren, "Unless you are circumcised according to the custom of Moses, you cannot be saved." 2 Therefore, when Paul and Barnabas had no small dissension and dispute with them, they determined that Paul and Barnabas and certain others of them should go up to Jerusalem, to the apostles and elders, about this question. 3 So, being sent on their way by the church, they passed through Phoenicia and Samaria, describing the conversion of the Gentiles; and they caused great joy to all the brethren. 4 And when they had come to Jerusalem, they were received by the church and the apostles and the elders; and they reported all things that God had done with them. 5 But some of the sect of the Pharisees who believed rose up, saying, "It is necessary to circumcise them, and to command them to keep the Law of Moses." 6 Now the apostles and elders came together to consider this matter.

When Paul and Barnabas were shepherding the church in Antioch, there arose a dispute about the necessity of circumcision. Though many of us have interpreted this disagreement as the Jewish Christians attempting to set up rules, there actually was some good thought behind it. To the Jews, especially the Messianic Jews, circumcision was a very significant mark for them. God established it as a sign of the everlasting Covenant—that God would bless us to make us a blessing. They more completely understood the gospel—that it was not just a transaction that guaranteed us to go to heaven when we die. Rather, it was to experience the full salvation of God while we were living the Covenant. Thus, while they understood that salvation was by grace through faith in Christ, they believed that it would also be a good idea to fulfill the mark given by God, with circumcision as an indicator that we are recipients of the Covenant. Though Paul was a learned Pharisee and certainly would have fully followed the prescription of circumcision as a Jew, he understood that salvation was only and solely through belief in Christ with nothing added, including the Mark of the Covenant. He explains in Colossians that it is not a physical mark but rather a mark of heart willfully surrendered to God and experiencing the life of the Covenant. As a result of this position, there arose a strong and legitimate disagreement between what the Messianic Jews believed and Paul and Barnabas. Fortunately, they all understood key things about disagreements:

1. Disagreements are okay, and not to be rejected per se.

2. They need to be resolved, with respect and honor.

3. Issues need to be processed until unity is reached—and unity is not just between those in disagreement but rather unity together with the Spirit. Taking the time to reach unity is important, regardless of how much time it takes.

As a result of this understanding, those that disagreed went together to the leadership of the apostles in Jerusalem. The apostles understood a key element of solving disagreements— listen and process both sides and then seek God's will. Both sides presented their positions; both listened to each other's position. Based on this open discussion, the apostles went to prayer and asked God to reveal His will. God revealed that being born again is purely based upon belief in Christ and only in Christ. Nothing, including the sign of the Covenant, was to be added as a requirement. So, Paul's position was correct. However he did not force his position nor fight against the other position. Both sides were willing to process the disagreement in honor and respect, seeking the will of God until they all received the unity of the Spirit. Furthermore, having reached unity, both sides then completely followed God's will, and did not maintain any resentment or opposition to God's will. They truly were in unity with each other and with God. (Please note that later, even Peter fell back into thinking circumcision was required, but Paul reminded him of God's will, and Peter responded positively to that challenge. This shows us that holding to one's beliefs is important in the process. We should never be afraid to express what we think, feel and believe, as long as we have a heart to listen to others positions and seek the will of God together.)

Rom. 12: 9–21:

9 Let love be without hypocrisy. Abhor what is evil. Cling to what is good. 10 Be kindly affectionate to one another with brotherly love, in honor giving preference to one another; 11 not lagging in diligence, fervent in spirit, serving the Lord; 12 rejoicing in hope, patient in tribulation, continuing steadfastly in prayer; 13 distributing to the needs of the saints, given to hospitality. 14 Bless those who persecute you; bless and do not curse. 15 Rejoice with those who rejoice, and weep with those who weep. 16 Be of the same mind toward one another. Do not set your mind on high things, but associate with the humble. Do not be wise in your own opinion. 17 Repay no one evil for evil. Have regard for good things in the sight of all men. 18 If it is possible, as much as depends on you, live peaceably with all men. 19 Beloved, do not avenge yourselves, but rather give place to wrath; for it is written, "Vengeance is Mine, I will repay," says the Lord. 20 Therefore "If your enemy is hungry, feed him; If he is thirsty, give him a drink; For in so doing you will heap coals of fire on his head."

God shows us something else important about conflict—that we are called to be at peace with everyone—AS FAR AS IT DEPENDS ON US—which means we are always to be in forgiveness and ready to reconcile our differences with respect and honor—with the purpose of reaching peace (shalom) with everyone. Does this mean that we will? No, because though we can pursue peace willingly, it always takes two people. Thus, both (or all) parties must have a heart to seek the will of God together, process their differences in a healthy way, then work together until they reach full unity with the Spirit (remember, it is available 100 percent of the time, every time). We cannot demand nor force the other party to seek peace and unity. It must be done willingly. What if the other party is unwilling to pursue reconciliation and unity? The Word tells us to let it go and believe "Vengeance is Mine, sayeth the Lord." This is a very profound truth and one that allows us to remain in peace, even when severe conflicts exist. We need never seek our own revenge (seek instead, how we might help someone settle what is "wrong and not just"). Why? Because of another important truth in Scripture. Genesis 12:1-3 says that God's Covenant is to bless us to make us a blessing. He then adds: "Blessed are those who bless us and cursed are those who curse us." Why? Because as Jesus spoke in Luke 10: 16: "The one who rejects you, rejects Me; and rejects the One (The Father) who sent Me." So, those who, because of pride, curse us and are unwilling to process our differences with honor and respect are thus cursed by God. He will establish true justice and set things straight. He asks us not to do this ourselves, but fully believe it shall be done (perhaps not in our timeframe or in our way, but for sure it will be done). What he asks us to do is, "bless them." This seems rather strange since He just told us that He is cursing them—so what does this mean? That our role is to pray that they might repent, since this is the only way anyone can prevent curses from God—actually the only way we are able to escape the curse of God—by repentance. So we are to pray as in 2 Timothy 2: 20—26: that they will come to their senses, be released from the will of Satan (pride and arrogance) and by their own will come back to repent. They then release the curse and return to blessing. So, when other people oppose us and will not process our disagreements in honor and respect, we are called by God to:

1. Go to forgiveness—on same basis as we have been forgiven (by His nature, though we deserved His wrath).

2. Let go and do not seek vengeance.

3. Understand that God will serve vengeance and bring curses upon those who oppose us.

4. Bless them by praying for them to repent.

5. Upon repentance, do not hold grudges. Instead, be willing to process the disagreements with honor and respect.

Another profound truth to all this: We must not be the ones who move to being cursed by refusing to process disagreements and conflicts with honor and respect. This truth is true for all, all the time. Thus, we need to remain humble, surrendered to seeking the will of the Father, and always be willing to process our issues with another, no matter how strongly we disagree. This is especially true for husbands and wives who are always called to seek unity together—100 percent of the time, every time. If we both do, we, nor our marriage, nor our family, nor our business, nor any aspect of our life will be cursed—but rather, we will blessed. It is up to us to choose to always pursue peace and the beauty of a life lived in unity. Remember that unity is never a forced agreement or a compromise, but rather, an honest process until unity with the Spirit is reached.

> *Ephesians. 4: 15–16; 25–32:*
>
> *15 but, speaking the truth in love, may grow up in all things into Him who is the head –Christ—16 from whom the whole body, joined and knit together by what every joint supplies, according to the effective working by which every part does its share, causes growth of the body for the edifying of itself in love.*
>
> *25 Therefore, putting away lying, "Let each one of you speak truth with his neighbor," for we are members of one another. 26 "Be angry, and do not sin": do not let the sun go down on your wrath, 27 nor give place to the devil. 28 Let him who stole steal no longer, but rather let him labor, working with his hands what is good, that he*

may have something to give him who has need. 29 Let no corrupt word proceed out of your mouth, but what is good for necessary edification, that it may impart grace to the hearers. 30 And do not grieve the Holy Spirit of God, by whom you were sealed for the day of redemption. 31 Let all bitterness, wrath, anger, clamor, and evil speaking be put away from you, with all malice. 32 And be kind to one another, tenderhearted, forgiving one another, just as God in Christ forgave you.

As we understand that resolving our disagreements is critical to reaching the blessed place of unity, we must learn an important secret to this process: speak the truth in love. Ephesians tells us that we are to be angry and sin not. Thus anger is not sin per se; and just anger can be defined as having our line of justice crossed by something or somebody. In order not to sin (i.e. move into the flesh and seek our own way, not God's), we are called to:

1. **Go to forgiveness**—even though they deserve our anger because of what has been done, we are to forgive them on the same basis that we have been forgiven: God's nature. Thus we can release the fact that we have been wronged or someone strongly disagrees with us, as we pursue a resolution that brings us back to unity.

2. **Ask the Father if my anger is justified**—perhaps my line of justice is not righteous and I am being unreasonable because of my own self-centeredness.

3. **Stay in the Spirit**—continue to desire to pursue God's will. My position may not be entirely correct or there is a new understanding that God wishes both of us to see together.

4. **Speak the truth in love**—the Scripture tells us not to let any unwholesome words come out of our mouths but only what will build up the other person by not grieving the Spirit but by speaking with respect and honor. Thus we are to calmly speak what we think, feel and believe is the truth for us. Our tone should not raise the emotional level of the discussion, but rather, provide an open forum for free back and forth discussion. As we share our truth, the other person is able to calmly share their truth as we both desire to seek God's truth, and His resolution that will bring us to agreement and unity. As we respectfully discourse back and forth, we will begin to understand the other person's viewpoints and their understanding of truth. Often, we might not be that far apart and can identify the specific points of our disagreement From there, we work toward a unified solution from God. As we get better at providing a safe environment for open discussion, the easier it is to process truth and then arrive at God's truth—which is best and none better.

1 Corinthians 1: 10:
10 Now I plead with you, brethren, by the name of our Lord Jesus Christ, that you all speak the same thing, and that there be no divisions among you, but that you be perfectly joined together in the same mind and in the same judgment.

Paul further tells us that God's will is certain. There is to be no division (dissension, schism) among us and that we must be perfectly (what ought to be, complete) joined together in the same mind, in the same judgment. Thus we are called to understand God's will together, and share the same opinion concerning what to do next—God's solution. Thus, we are called, as one of our highest relationship priorities, especially marriage, to take the time to work through our differences so that no division keeps us from the unity of God's will.

1 Kings 3: 5–9:
5 At Gibeon the Lord appeared to Solomon in a dream by night; and God said, "Ask! What shall I give you?" 6 And Solomon said: "You have shown great mercy to Your servant David my father, because he walked before You in truth, in righteousness, and in uprightness of heart with You; You have continued this great kindness for him, and You have given him a son to sit on his throne, as it is this day. 7 Now, O Lord my God, You have made Your servant king instead of my father David, but I am a little child; I do not know how to go out or come in. 8 And Your servant is in the midst of Your people whom You have chosen, a great people, too numerous to be numbered or counted. 9 Therefore give to Your servant an understanding heart to judge Your people, that I may discern between good and evil. For who is able to judge this great people of Yours?"

Another key to this process is to ask God for a hearing heart so that we can correctly discern between good and evil. Most of us see evil as dark black and demonic. However, the Hebrew words here mean something different—things that are hard, difficult, oppressive, frustrating, annoying, irritating, against us, and unpleasant. The things that are obviously dark and black are easy to discern. However, when things look pretty good or are gray, we need discernment from God. Through His insight and truth, our lives can be characterized by good and not by things that constantly frustrate and annoy us. As we both seek God's will together, it is important that we are abiding in the Vine, hearing His voice, and allowing new discernment to be spoken to us together, so that we see what He sees.

Proverbs 8: 32–35:

32 *"Now therefore, listen to me, my children, For blessed
are those who keep my ways.* **33** *Hear instruction and be
wise, And do not disdain it.* **34** *Blessed is the man who
listens to me, Watching daily at my gates, Waiting at the
posts of my doors.* **35** *For whoever finds me finds life, And
obtains favor from the Lord;*

Stay in Process together. As we process disagreements, we
often come to a place that seems to offer no solution. This is
important to understand because unity with God is neither
compromise nor negotiation. It is staying with the process
until we both see what God wants us to see. When we come
to these places without solutions,, Linda and I just understand
that we, as of yet, do not know God's will. We do not let our
disagreement ruin our evening, our weekend, or our week. We
just set it aside and together pray that God would show us His
solution. We practice the truths taught in Proverbs chapter 8:

1. **Listen:** we will be sensitive to hearing new insight
   and discernment and learning God's perspective as He
   speaks to us spiritually. We both have asked for and
   received a hearing heart—so we have the ability to hear
   what He says. We expect to hear His voice so we listen
   carefully. Together we follow what He speaks (definition of obedience).

2. **Watch:** we often specifically perform our due diligence
   and ask further questions, seek new information, and
   receive new facts about our issue. As we observe, the
   Lord is working to bring these new facts to life to reveal
   to us answers that we as yet do not know.

3. **Wait:** we understand that we are not to act prematurely
   by moving ahead of God's answer. Since we do not yet

know God's will in unity, we've learned that waiting is best. Often, this is because God's timing is critical. The Revelation needed is purposely being withheld from us because of His timing. We have learned that His timing is absolutely best and not to force our timing in any way. This means that if there is a deadline in the situation, when we are not in unity, we must let the deadline pass and that alone was God's will.

Proverbs 11: 14; 15:22:
11:14 *Where there is no counsel, the people fall; But in the multitude of counselors there is safety.*

15:22 *Without counsel, plans go awry, But in the multitude of counselors they are established.*

Have other counselors join us in the process. We are not seeking their opinion or advice. Rather, we are in need of godly counselors who are willing to walk with us and process things together in the Spirit. We need their help confirming God's answers or providing new input to the process—mostly through good questions or networking us to experts. This is especially important if we are bogged down and can't seem to get past our disagreement. We should never be ashamed to admit that we are stuck and to bring in Godly counselors to assist us in moving to unity. Since they have no vested interest in the outcome of our discussions, they can see things more objectively and don't take sides. Rather, they help us understand the truth and seek God's will instead of our own. This process is not about asking lots of other believers their opinions. It's about having one or two people around us that we know walk in the Spirit, abide in Christ, and hear His voice. Their role is to bring new insight and revelation from the Spirit, and provide confirmation of our movement toward unified solutions. We are never to put them in the position as being God themselves (and thus, always having the answer). We should see them for what they are, fellow travelers who the Lord is using to bring us to unity.

> ### John 8: 28–32, 36:
> **28** *Then Jesus said to them, "When you lift up the Son of Man, then you will know that I am He, and that I do nothing of Myself; but as My Father taught Me, I speak these things.* **29** *And He who sent Me is with Me. The Father has not left Me alone, for I always do those things that please Him." 30 As He spoke these words, many believed in Him. 31 Then Jesus said to those Jews who believed Him, "If you abide in My word, you are My disciples indeed. 32 And you shall know the truth, and the truth shall make you free." ...36 Therefore if the Son makes you free, you shall be free indeed.*

The only way to know truth is to abide in Christ words: Without abiding individually in the Word of God, our hearts become self-centered and hardened and our ability to process disagreements diminishes. We will lose our desire to know truth and only persuade the other party of our position, which may not be true at all. Thus in order to experience the freedom of unity, we must be abiding in the Word knowing that this will lead us to truth. It is a prerequisite to seeking and knowing truth, and is an absolute that cannot be ignored. Abiding, abiding, abiding. It may be that before we continue our elevated level of disagreement and our position becoming harder, we are called to **Psalm 4: 4–5:**

> **4** *Be angry, and do not sin. Meditate within your heart on your bed, and be still. Selah 5 Offer the sacrifices of righteousness, And put your trust in the Lord.*

Separate, go to our own place, and get our hearts right with God. This requires forgiveness (remember though, they may deserve our anger but we can be forgiving on the same basis that we had been forgiven—not what we deserve, but God's nature). Go back to abiding in the Vine—in His Word and in the Spirit to have our heart softened to seek God's will, not our own. When we are in a state of abiding, we can go back to processing truth together with the other party. What Linda and I do is after having separated to get our hearts right, we come back together and ask each other if we are okay to talk. We understand that this means that our anger has been released and that we can calmly, with respect and honor, talk through the issues of our disagreement. If our emotions are still running high and we haven't returned to a peaceful state with God, we wait for God's answer.

Conflict and disagreement are normal and actually are to be embraced. I learned that it is particularly important for Linda to maintain her integrity until God shows us in unity the resolution to our disagreements. As I stated above, we see disagreements, not as problems to be forced by either one of us, but rather to understand that we just do not yet know God's will. So it does not ruin our night, our week or weekend. We simply table things until we reach agreement. We follow these principles carefully, as we process with respect and honor through our disagreement to reach unity. Because we have committed to only make decisions when we are in unity, we are able to comfortably process our issues until we reach unity.

For example, we were faced with making a decision about our calendar, including some travel opportunities, both for business and ministry. As someone who can spin multiple plates at once, I saw no problem in our schedule—in fact, I found it stimulating. Linda, on the other hand, who does not handle multiple plates at once well, was overwhelmed by the schedule. We both saw our own personal truth about it and held those thoughts and feelings going into our discussions. We shared our individual thoughts, understood that we disagreed, and without rancor or hardness, knew that we just did not yet know God's will. We agreed to pray and come back to process new thoughts and information. Linda was able to articulate why the schedule was going to be so oppressive to her. She saw that the travel would be valuable for both our ministry and business, but she was still stressed by the commitment. As I prayed, I began to fully understand her heart and emotion, and saw that, in fact, the schedule was overwhelming. I had to maintain integrity with the things that I saw as important, so I processed through the things that were most important for her to join and what things I could possibly do alone or skip altogether. We kept seeking the truth and processed until we finally saw the schedule God had in mind. We both confirmed it in the Spirit, to unity and saw how beautiful the answer was. It was exactly when and where God wanted us to serve and where not to serve. It maintained our priority of marriage and honored each other in the process. We did disagree, but worked through in a healthy way to a God-given solution.

Another example is where I ignored these principles and suffered the consequences. Every two to three years we purchase a new car for Linda. We always buy a one-year-old car to avoid the large first-year value depreciation. We found a wonderful Ford Explorer, which she was excited to receive. We negotiated a contract and then ordered some after-market upgrades that the dealer would install. A few days later, I received a phone call from the dealer telling me that they noticed the fuel pump was damaged; would I mind waiting an extra couple days while they replace it. I said, "No problem." When they finally delivered the car to Linda, she noticed some scratches and discoloration where previously there had been none. She refused to accept the car and asked for the ticket back, which they did. The dealer called me and said it was just some overzealous polishers and that they would get it completed and fixed up. Since we had already paid for the car, I agreed. Linda felt that there was something not quite right and that we should not accept this particular car. I then violated everything that we teach. I said it'll be no problem and let's accept the car since they will be able to fix it. I was focused more on the avoidance of the hassle of doing it all over as opposed to a particular problem with this car. They again delivered the car, which now seemed okay. I accepted it, over Linda's objection. She said there was something wrong and that her spirit was not at peace. At that moment I should have followed what we knew to be true and that was to process further together until we received unity in the Spirit. For expediency's sake and because of my selfishness, I did not. A few days later Linda took the car to a carwash. Water from the carwash hit her in the back of the head as it was flooding in from the back door. There were holes all over. She took it to another local Ford dealer to complain and to ask them to fix it. This dealer fixed the holes. As she was driving away, the entire front panel fell off. She took it back to the dealer and said that now they have damaged the front panel. This dealer looked carefully at the car and said: "Lady, this car is damaged all over. You really need to take it to a body shop." She took it to a body shop who evaluated the entire car and said that almost everything on the car has been replaced including many parts of the engine and most of the panels. He showed her the barcodes of all the parts that had been replaced. He said that it looked like the car had fallen off a lift and that they had to replace everything damaged in the fall. When she brought it home, and related the story, I was furious. I called the original dealer and said that there's been damage to this car, which we can prove and I would like to bring it back for him to replace it with a different car. This dealer refused and offered that I go ahead and sue him. In Colorado there is a government agency to deal specifically with car dealer fraud, so I filed a report and requested an investigation. A month later, the investigator said that he could see all the damage to the car but there was no proof in any of the records in any system and thus, I was out of luck. I was explaining the story in a retreat where one participant was a local lawyer, He said he would take up the case and not charge me anything because we could not allow a dealer to behave in this manner. I was grateful for an answered prayer, and began to work on preparing the suit.

As I was preparing, the Lord spoke to me and asked, "What are you doing? Look at 1 Corinthians 6 and see what I have to say about what you're doing." I did and recognized that I was active in the flesh (as I had been during the whole process) and not the Spirit. So, I stopped pursuing the suit and asked Linda if she could put up with the car for a year as by then, we probably could break even. She said, "No way." I asked if we could switch cars and let me live with this problem for the year. She again refused. So, I went to the Lord and asked Him what to do. He said to buy her a new car. I answered, "Yeah, but this is going to cost me a lot of money." He said, "Yes, $8,000—how is this working out for you?" I said: "I got it." I had my son who negotiates our car deals process with Linda to buy a new car. He asked me for my bottom line in negotiation. I said it doesn't matter, tell the dealer about the damage, and do your best—I expect an $8,000 loss. It was. Linda loves the new car. I share this to reveal that the process works on both sides. If we are too selfish or too busy to go to unity, we are going to suffer the consequences. If we're willing to process through unity and, in this case, I would have seen God's will was not to accept the car, we would've experienced God's best. The process works and I can testify that it is way better to go to unity then to skip the proper steps to get to unity. Ouch.

CHAPTER 7
Praying Through to Unity

As we seek God's answers to our conflicts, especially when we do not usually come to a unified resolution with God, we are called to go to prayer.

James 1: 5–8:

5 If any of you lacks wisdom, let him ask of God, who gives to all liberally and without reproach, and it will be given to him. 6 But let him ask in faith, with no doubting, for he who doubts is like a wave of the sea driven and tossed by the wind. 7 For let not that man suppose that he will receive anything from the Lord; 8 he is a double-minded man, unstable in all his ways.

Ask God for Wisdom: James tells us that when we lack wisdom (by definition when we do not have a unified solution), we are to ask God who will answer us generously. The Greek word here means *with great clarity, without finding fault*. He does not focus on who or what is wrong, but rather on bringing about a solution that answers our specific conflict. However, there is a condition—that we both believe we will receive and accept His answer. We do not have to understand fully the answer itself— that may take further processing—but we must believe that we will hear from Him, or, for some reason known only to God,

He cannot tell us. There is a very practical reason for this. If we do not believe that we will hear His answer, then we will process any new input in confusion, continually wondering whether it came from Him, from us or from the enemy. We must settle on the fact that we will hear from Him and that it will be His solution. It is important to note that it is not dependent on our spiritual maturity. Thus, hearing from God is not dependent upon us growing in our ability to hear His voice. Rather, He will adjust His ability to communicate to us at any level. For example I have two grandsons, ages eleven and eight. The eleven-year-old is accelerating in his intellectual understanding at the moment. They can both ask me the same question and I can give them an answer. The eleven-year-old can say he understands it while the eight-year-old might say he has no idea what I just said. I do not tell him that he should wait three years for an answer until he has the ability to understand my explanation. Instead, I adjust my communication to his level so that he does understand my answer today. God takes responsibility to adjust His communication to us to fit our particular level of spiritual maturity. It is a wonderful promise given to us and all we have to do is believe that He will.

1 Kings 10: 1–3:
1 Now when the queen of Sheba heard of the fame of Solomon concerning the name of the Lord, she came to test him with hard questions. 2 She came to Jerusalem with a very great retinue, with camels that bore spices, very much gold, and precious stones; and when she came to Solomon, she spoke with him about all that was in her heart. 3 So Solomon answered all her questions; there was nothing so difficult for the king that he could not explain it to her.

Come with every hard question: Another important factor to understand is that no conflict or disagreement is too grand or difficult for God to resolve. When the Queen of Sheba visited Solomon, the Bible says she brought every difficult question that was in her heart as she sought to test his wisdom. Solomon answered them all. Nothing was beyond his ability, because God was giving him the answers. Thus God has an open invitation for us to bring Him every difficult and sticky question. By His promise, we know He will provide an answer. This releases us from having to figure this out on our own, or stopping short of a correct answer by acting too soon, according to our own will. Thus even when we have a severe disagreement or a seemingly insurmountable roadblock to overcome, we should go together to God in prayer and expect that He will provide the answer.

Hebrews 10: 19–25; 35–11:3

10: 19 Therefore, brethren, having boldness to enter the Holiest by the blood of Jesus, 20 by a new and living way which He consecrated for us, through the veil, that is, His flesh, 21 and having a High Priest over the house of God, 22 let us draw near with a true heart in full assurance of faith, having our hearts sprinkled from an evil conscience and our bodies washed with pure water. 23 Let us hold fast the confession of our hope without wavering, for He who promised is faithful. 24 And let us consider one another in order to stir up love and good works, 25 not forsaking the assembling of ourselves together, as is the manner of some, but exhorting one another, and so much the more as you see the Day approaching.

35 Therefore do not cast away your confidence, which has great reward. 36 For you have need of endurance, so that after you have done the will of God, you may receive the promise: 37 "For yet a little while, And He who is coming will come and will not tarry. 38 Now the just shall live by faith; But if anyone draws back, My soul has no pleasure in him." **39** *But we are not of those who draw back to perdition, but of those who believe to the saving of the soul.*

11:1 *Now faith is the substance of things hoped for, the evidence of things not seen.* **2** *For by it the elders obtained a good testimony.* **3** *By faith we understand that the worlds were framed by the word of God, so that the things that are seen were not made of things that are visible.*

Go with confidence and boldness to prayer: This goes in line with one of our greatest privileges—being able to enter directly into His throne room and discuss our disagreement with God. In Hebrews it is revealed that the veil that separated the holy of holies from everyone else has been opened. We must understand the symbolism of this. The temple was segregated into different courts and enclosed areas. First, was the court of Gentiles, where non-Jews who had a heart for God could gather and seek to worship Him. Then there was the court of women followed by the court of men. Next, there was the court of priests who were the ministers between God and man. Farthest inside was the holy of holies—where only the high priest could enter—and he could only enter once a year. It was so sacred that they tied a rope around his legs so that if perchance he died in the holy of holies, he could be dragged out since no one else could enter. The high priest would go to the veil which was an eighty-foot-high curtain eight-inches thick separating the holy of holies from the court of the priest. He would enter once a year on the Day of Atonement, and sacrifice an unblemished animal for himself first, to be cleansed, then one for his family to be cleansed and a third one for the nation of Israel and those that had a heart for God.

The Holy of Holies was separated from the rest of the tabernacle/temple by the veil—a huge, heavy drape made of fine linen and blue, purple and scarlet yarn and embroidered with gold cherubim. God said that He would appear in the Holy of Holies (Leviticus 16:2); hence, the need for the veil.

In the Holy of Holies were these items:

1. The *aron* (The Ark of the Covenant), which contained the tablets (the second set, as well as the shards of the first tablets).

2. The Foundation Stone, upon which the ark sat.

3. Aaron's staff (see Numbers 17:16–26).

4. The jar of manna (see Exodus 16:33–34).

5. The Torah scroll that Moses wrote immediately before his passing (see Deuteronomy 31:26).

The Holy of Holies was entered once a year by the High Priest on the Day of Atonement, to sprinkle the blood of sacrificial animals (a bull offered as atonement for the Priest and his household, and a goat offered as atonement for the people) and offer incense upon the Ark of the Covenant and the mercy seat which sat on top of the ark in the First Temple (the Second Temple had no ark and the blood was sprinkled where the Ark would have been and the incense was left on the Foundation Stone). The animal was sacrificed on the Brazen Altar and the blood was carried into the most holy place. The golden censers were also found in the Most Holy Place.

There was no seat, as the high priest could only stand and offer the sacrifice, which was good for only one year. When Christ died on the cross, the veil was rent in two from top to bottom and He entered the throne room with the Father and sat at His right hand. He was able to sit because the sacrificing was finished once and for all, it would never have to be repeated again. Thus, Christ served as both the high priest who could enter the holy of holies and the sacrificial lamb that completed the atonement on our behalf. Those that now believe that He died for our sins and was resurrected, raised to the right hand of the Father, now have direct access to the throne room. We have been given this privilege through the blood of Christ and the resurrection. There is no other condition. This is wonderful news. We don't have to be holy, nor perfect, nor fully walking in the Spirit to be allowed to walk into God's throne room. Rather, the Bible says we are to go with great confidence and boldness, coming with an authentic heart. The Father desires for us to talk to Him directly, without partiality to share what is truly on our heart. Thus He invites us to come together with our disagreements and conflicts, and with great confidence and boldness, march directly to the throne and ask Him for answers and solutions. He does not ask us to go figure things out ourselves or to resolve them and negotiate them. Rather, He says He has the answers and that we are to take advantage of this wonderful privilege to march in any time to ask Him for His help.

He further encourages to not waste this opportunity—in fact, The Word says we will be rewarded for coming. The Greek words here actually say He will pay us to come (receive His amazing answers that reveal His solutions to our issues). And that it requires faith—certainty faith in what He says to be true, since the material (the world) was created by the Spiritual—what He spoke. We are called to this wonderful gift of prayer in the throne room and to faith, as follows:

1. Enter with boldness—no limitations.

2. Share our authentic heart—what we think, feel, and believe.

3. Ask for wisdom.

4. Listen to what He speaks—His Rhema Word to us.

5. Go to faith by abiding with Him until believed.

6. Expect it to happen.

And it all starts with prayer!! Why would we not?

Luke 11: 2–13:
2 So He said to them, "When you pray, say: Our Father in heaven, Hallowed be Your name. Your kingdom come. b Your will be done On earth as it is in heaven. 3 Give us day by day our daily bread. 4 And forgive us our sins, For we also forgive everyone who is indebted to us. And do not lead us into temptation, But deliver us from the evil one." 5 And He said to them, "Which of you shall have a friend, and go to him at midnight and say to him, 'Friend, lend me three loaves; 6 for a friend of mine has come to me on his journey, and I have nothing to set before him'; 7 and he will answer from within and say, 'Do not trouble me; the door is now shut, and my children are with me in bed; I cannot rise and give to you'? 8 I say to you, though he will not rise and give to him because he is his friend, yet because of his persistence he will rise and give him as many as he needs. 9 "So I say to you, ask, and it will be given to you; seek, and you will find; knock, and it will be opened to you. 10 For everyone who asks receives, and he who seeks finds, and to him who knocks it will be opened. 11 If a son asks for bread from any father among you, will he give him a stone? Or if he asks for a fish, will he give him a serpent instead of a fish? 12 Or if he asks for an egg, will he offer him a scorpion? 13 If you then, being evil, know how to give good gifts to your children, how much more will your heavenly Father give the Holy Spirit to those who ask Him!"

As we seek answers, we are to pray in the manner that Christ taught us—asking for His kingdom to come, for His will to be done. If it were automatic He would not have told us to ask for it. As we ask he tells us the story of the friend who was knocking at a door at midnight. He knocked until he received an answer. The friend said he did not give an answer because he was his friend but rather because of his persistence. Since we are asking for God's will, it cannot mean that we ask, ask, ask until we get what we want—rather that we ask until we receive an answer.

In the story, had the friend said to come back the next morning and he would receive bread then the person knocking on the door would have stopped and known that he had not received the answer he hoped for and would have come back the next day. So persistence is not wearing God down, but rather to stay with the process until we fully understand God's will. **We are to ask, seek information and knock.** 'Ask' is backing up a step and asking for the will of the Father. Often our prayers are just a list asking God to do something. We don't fully appreciate that prayer is also intended for us to hear what He wants to do. Thus we should ask for His will, not ours.

Second we seek information as if it were lost treasure. This is our role of due diligence and seeking more data and information—until we see the truth. It would be as if someone told you there were ten gold bars hidden in your house but did not tell you exactly where. Based upon that, you would seek it by looking under every cushion, piece of furniture, in closets etc. until you found them all. That should be the picture of our seeking. We should never be afraid to continually seek new information, new data and new insight until we fully receive God's will. This is another reason why it is so important to process things together because the other party may hold pieces of information that we don't have. Then we are to knock as opportunity presents itself to see if this is the specific answer to God's will.

If we knock and it opens and we are to understand that this is God's will or even perhaps that this is just another hallway to the next piece of God's will. If the door closes, we are not to knock it down but to recognize that there is more to be understood and that we are to go further in pursuing His will. Jesus tells us further that he will not bait and switch us. If we ask for His will He will not make us guess at it or think it is one thing when it is really something else. In fact he says He is giving us the ultimate gift, the Holy Spirit, whose role is to show us the will of God. So in our prayer life, particularly when we are at a place of disagreement, if we pray together He says He will give us His answer and we will then know in unity His will is best and none better.

1 John 5: 14–15:
14 Now this is the confidence that we have in Him, that if we ask anything according to His will, He hears us. 15 And if we know that He hears us, whatever we ask, we know that we have the petitions that we have asked of Him.

Ask according to His will: He further tells us that if we ask according to His will, He hears us and promises to answer our prayer. We can expect God to fulfill what He has spoken. Often we focus on what we need to do to bring resolution. Actually it is about what He wishes to do to demonstrate His magnificent will to us.

John 15: 7–8:
If you abide in Me, and My words abide in you, you will ask what you desire, and it shall be done for you. 8 By this My Father is glorified, that you bear much fruit; so you will be My disciples.

Ask what He is promising to us: This is reinforced by the amazing truth that if we abide in Him and His words (what He has spoken according to His will) abide in us, we can pray it and the Father will perform it; by this He glorifies Himself and we bear witness to His wonderful work. Thus, His will is more about His promises to us as opposed to what we are to do for Him. When we make this shift, we begin to recognize that he lifts us out of our natural thinking which leads to disagreements. We begin to seek His grand will, which is His supernatural work in our lives that brings the full resolution to our disagreements. This also releases us from the pressure of having to figure things out and pursuing our own way. Life is intended to be experienced through His miraculous work in our circumstances and situations and that we are to bear witness to His intervention to others—bringing glory to Him.

> *John 14: 12–14:*
> *12 "Most assuredly, I say to you, he who believes in Me, the works that I do he will do also; and greater works than these he will do, because I go to My Father. 13 And whatever you ask in My name, that I will do, that the Father may be glorified in the Son. 14 If you ask anything in My name, I will do it.*

Pray with His authority to us: As we pray according to His will, we further have the privilege of praying in His name—under the authority that He has given us to join in His greater supernatural works. As we pursue unity, especially through our differences of opinion, He wants us to recognize that He is drawing us to a much higher level. He is inviting us to experience and bear witness to works that only He can accomplish—supernatural and miraculous. Thus, we don't hold this authority in our own power, but rather as representatives to whom He has delegated His authority through what He has spoken to us. This would be similar to a president of a company who reports to a Board of Directors. Since he represents the company, under the authority of the Board of Directors, he cannot decide on his own to sign a multimillion-dollar contract to buy a building that he thinks is a good idea. He does not have that authority. Rather, he must receive authority through a proclamation of the board. With the proclamation in hand, he then has the authority to obligate the company to purchase this multimillion-dollar building.

It's the same for followers of Christ. Christ holds the authority, which has been given to Him by the Father. He delegates this authority to us as He speaks promises and clarifies His will—what He wants to do supernaturally, His greater works. Our prayer life is intended to elevate us to a higher place where we are not asking God to do things for us, but rather we understand that He is inviting us to join Him in what He wants to do for us. As we receive this authority, we are privileged to be able to exercise it in specific situations and circumstances that we face—for which we have sought wisdom. This is especially important when we experience disagreements. Again He does not wish us to negotiate our own solution, but rather to see Him and His grander solutions.

Luke 9: 1–2: 10: 1–13, 16–20:
9:1 Then He called His twelve disciples together and gave them power and authority over all demons, and to cure diseases. 2 He sent them to preach the kingdom of God and to heal the sick.

10:1 After these things the Lord appointed seventy others also, and sent them two by two before His face into every city and place where He Himself was about to go. 2 Then He said to them, "The harvest truly is great, but the laborers are few; therefore pray the Lord of the harvest to send out laborers into His harvest. 3 Go your way; behold, I send you out as lambs among wolves. 4 Carry neither moneybag, knapsack, nor sandals; and greet no one along the road. 5 But whatever house you enter, first say, 'Peace to this house.' 6 And if a son of peace is there, your peace will rest on it; if not, it will return to you. 7 And remain in the same house, eating and drinking such things as they give, for the laborer is worthy of his wages. Do not go from house to house. 8 Whatever city you enter, and they receive you, eat such things as are set before you. 9 And heal the sick there, and say to them, 'The kingdom of God has come near to you.' 10 But whatever city you enter, and they do not receive you, go out into its streets and say,

11 'The very dust of your city which clings to us we wipe off against you. Nevertheless know this, that the kingdom of God has come near you.' 12 But I say to you that it will be more tolerable in that Day for Sodom than for that city. 13 "Woe to you, Chorazin! Woe to you, Bethsaida! For if the mighty works which were done in you had been done in Tyre and Sidon, they would have repented long ago, sitting in sackcloth and ashes

16 He who hears you hears Me, he who rejects you rejects Me, and he who rejects Me rejects Him who sent Me." 17 Then the seventy returned with joy, saying, "Lord, even the demons are subject to us in Your name." 18 And He said to them, "I saw Satan fall like lightning from heaven. 19 Behold, I give you the authority to trample on serpents and scorpions, and over all the power of the enemy, and nothing shall by any means hurt you. 20 Nevertheless do not rejoice in this, that the spirits are subject to you, but rather rejoice because your names are written in heaven."

Be faithful to the authority given to us: He gives us this authority specifically in order to carry out His supernatural work in the places we are being sent. It is interesting to note that he sends us two-by-two—fully understanding that unity in understanding His will is the gateway to the supernatural. Further we are to claim that the supernatural work is demonstrating the very kingdom of God, in which we are living and where we are reaching unity. He further teaches that if we meet resistance, that we have to take back what we have offered (which implies that we have peace ourselves) and dust our feet off. This means we are not to work at persuading those around us to experience the same supernatural works as we do—rather to just teach them that the gateway is to the Spirit.

1 Corinthians 14: 1–5:

1 Pursue love, and desire spiritual gifts, but especially that you may prophesy. 2 For he who speaks in a tongue does not speak to men but to God, for no one understands him; however, in the spirit he speaks mysteries. 3 But he who prophesies speaks edification and exhortation and comfort to men. 4 He who speaks in a tongue edifies himself, but he who prophesies edifies the church. 5 I wish you all spoke with tongues, but even more that you prophesied; for he who prophesies is greater than he who speaks with tongues, unless indeed he interprets, that the church may receive edification.

Learn the prophetic gift: One of the key elements of our privilege of walking with God, is the gift of prophecy. Prophecy has two significant meanings: **forth telling**—speaking God's truth and understanding how it relates to current situations; and **foretelling**—telling what is yet to come. He instructs us to especially request this gift and to use it in our relationships with others, especially those near to us and, most-particularly, our spouses. Thus, we are seeking God's answers to the very questions of our life. Together, we are to go to a prayer of prophecy that asks God to reveal for the moment as well as for the future. He tells us that this will have specific qualities:

1. Edification—for purpose of building up.

2. Exhortation—instructing, informing, guiding, challenging.

3. Comfort—encouragement, hope, positive truth of God's will.

As we are hearing from God, the nature of what He speaks is always intended to reveal His good plans and His good solutions for the issues and circumstances of our life. It may be challenging, but it is never harsh or condemning. God is always inviting us to join Him in His great work. Together as we seek this gift, we practice listening and processing in our times of prayer, as follows:

1. Take one issue, decision or question at a time.

2. Write in your journals what you know to be true already, and what you think, feel and believe about this particular situation.

3. Write in your journals what you need to know or understand as you are pursuing God's will.

4. Discuss any new insight, revelation or word that you have received in the Spirit.

5. Go to prayer together, asking God to reveal what further He has to say about this particular situation.

6. Spend two to five-minutes in silence and be aware of any pictures, thoughts, words, ideas, visions, or anything else that the Lord wishes to reveal.

7. Write down what you saw or heard.

8. Write down any insight and revelation about what you saw or heard.

9. Share together what you saw or heard.

10. Discuss your insight revelation and interpretation of what has been revealed.

11. Move into further watching, listening and waiting. Move into a seek-not mode as you are processing the prophetic revelations that the Lord is speaking.

Remember that God's revelation is step-by-step and will not necessarily be very detailed. Though we would like everything set out clearly for the next many months, the Lord desires our fellowship through our daily dependence on walking with Him. Though we prefer end solutions to our questions, the Lord provides step-by-step solutions. As long as we are alive, we realize that no solution is actually final. They are always only a gateway to the next place in our walk with Him.

Matthew 18: 18–20:
18 Assuredly, I say to you, whatever you bind on earth will be bound in heaven, and whatever you loose on earth will be loosed in heaven. 19 Again I say to you that if two of you agree on earth concerning anything that they ask, it will be done for them by My Father in heaven. 20 For where two or three are gathered together in My name, I am there in the midst of them."

Stay with it until you reach unity! In our prayer life, He tells us that as we gather in His name (come together to seek His will and understand His work under His authority) we are called to come to unity with the Spirit where everyone involved sees exactly what He sees. This is what unity looks like. It is neither a negotiation nor a compromise. Rather, it is a peace-filled confirmation in our spirits that our solution is His solution. We are then called to boldly pray the solution, including the power to bind the work of the enemy, so that he becomes completely disarmed and we loose the very power of heaven into the situation. What a wonderful "checker" to our decisions. Seek unity—stay with it until received—and then when received together, we'll recognize His will, (What He promises to do and what He invites us step-by-step to do) and can boldly expect it to be fulfilled.

Two of our children, Peter and Michelle, lead one of our businesses—a medical transportation business. We were experiencing a rather difficult client, who was asking us to reduce our pricing. We had already absorbed significant cost to serve them and keep their business. In fact, we saved them over $2 million annually. We were stuck with either losing the business or performing the service for a minimal margin. We all came together and went to prophetic prayer. We all received a different message. God had promised us the Covenant that we would retain the client. We were to experience a new thing, and to seek His creativity. With that truth, we went back to further prophetic prayer. There, He revealed to us a new design that would meet the service requirements and be able to reduce our costs. It was truly remarkable. It worked so well we were able to retain the client and carry out the changes. We realize that we have the great privilege of access to God, who sees all and knows all, can communicate truth to us and teach us how to solve our problems. We realized further that we were to seek His solutions in unity and desire His will, versus trying to figure it out. We can all attest to the magnificence of ask, seek and knock, and continuing the process until we see and understand God's answers.

Another couple at one of our retreats, owned a once wonderful business that, due to changes in the product and services provided by their vendors, was suddenly losing money They were experiencing severe cash flow issues and wondered if, in fact, the business could even continue. They each held different opinions, but knew that going to God in unity was the key. They went to prophetic prayer, and heard God speak to them that he would save their business and give them victory. They abided in those promises for many months, even though it appeared that the business was getting worse. Their faith was being tested. They continued to pray and stand by what they'd heard. Then a new vendor came with a new product and they were able to tremendously increase their cash flow. During this time, they were forced to streamline their operations and later recognized that this was the purpose for the entire exercise. They needed to become much more efficient in the back room so that they could meet the demands of the market going forward. It's been a wonderful process to see, as God has spoken His promises and ask us to believe. He honors His promises.

Another couple experienced something similar. They were considering purchasing a large tract of land in a different state for retirement—to use as a family gathering place for great memories and to lead retreats. One such property was viable, but only "just barely." At one of our retreats, we all went to prophetic prayer together and heard that God would deliver this property to them. They received a specific promise out of Exodus and we confirmed it in unity. As time progressed, many more difficulties arose. It seemed at each step it was more unlikely that they would receive this property. However, together we stayed in unity and prayed that God would fulfill His promise. He did. They received it and are on their way toward building a grand place. Plus, they can fully bear witness to the beauty of hearing God's answers, standing on His promises, and staying in unity in belief until the promise is received. It was a phenomenal process to be part of and to see how this couple stayed in unity through the entire ordeal.

CHAPTER 8
Biblical Examples of Unity

Read through the following Biblical stories to see how the Concept of Unity is applied to understand and follow God's Will—especially what He promises to do in light of a certain situation. These will help you see how these truths are played out in real situations and then can apply to your own.

1 Samuel 23: 1–13:

1 Then they told David, saying, "Look, the Philistines are fighting against Keilah, and they are robbing the threshing floors." 2 Therefore David inquired of the Lord, saying, "Shall I go and attack these Philistines?" And the Lord said to David, "Go and attack the Philistines, and save Keilah." 3 But David's men said to him, "Look, we are afraid here in Judah. How much more then if we go to Keilah against the armies of the Philistines?" 4 Then David inquired of the Lord once again. And the Lord answered him and said, "Arise, go down to Keilah. For I will deliver the Philistines into your hand. 5 And David and his men went to Keilah and fought with the Philistines, struck them with a mighty blow, and took away their livestock. So David saved the inhabitants of Keilah. 6 Now it happened, when Abiathar the son of Ahimelech fled to David at Keilah, that he went down with an ephod in his hand. 7 And Saul was told that David had gone to Keilah. So Saul said, "God has delivered him into my hand, for he has shut himself in by entering a town that has gates and bars." 8 Then Saul called all the people together for war, to go down to Keilah to besiege David and his men. 9 When David knew that Saul plotted evil against him, he said to Abiathar the priest, "Bring the ephod here." 10 Then David said, "O Lord God of Israel, Your servant has certainly heard that Saul seeks to come to Keilah to destroy the city for my sake. 11 Will the men of Keilah deliver me into his hand? Will Saul come down, as Your servant has heard? O Lord God of Israel, I pray, tell Your servant." And the Lord said, "He will come down." 12 Then David said, "Will the men of Keilah deliver me and my men into the hand of Saul?" And the Lord said, "They will deliver you." 13 So David and his men, about six hundred, arose and departed from Keilah and went wherever they could go. Then it was told Saul that David had escaped from Keilah; so he halted the expedition.

The context here is concerning David and his mighty men. David had already been ordained and anointed by Samuel as king of Israel. He had already defeated Goliath and was victorious in every battle he fought. He was so successful that Saul became jealous and, knowing that David had been anointed as heir apparent, sought to kill him. David had fled and wound up in a cave all alone. He laments in Psalm 142 that he did not understand why God's promises were not being fulfilled for him—he was all alone and certainly had not been established as king. His family sought him out and comforted him. God told David to build an army from among the lowest level of citizens of Israel, the debtors and unskilled. (Note that the fulfillment of God's promises are in line with us being faithful to small things, as we, step-by-step, walk into the fullness of

His promises). David molded these men into an army of six-hundred mighty men of war. Saul was not deterred since his army was much larger and could easily defeat David and his men. As a result, David hid out in caves, moving from place to place to avoid being captured. One day, while he was hiding, , he received word that a nearby town, Keilah, was under attack by the Philistines. David inquired of the Lord and asked if he should go and save the town. God said yes. David then went to his men and said that God had spoken. They were to go save Keilah. The men reacted negatively. They reasoned that they weren't strong enough to help and were close to being captured by Saul. They said no. This was a critical moment for unity. David could either accept their reasoning and stayed hidden (which was logical), or he could have forced his will on the man saying that God had spoken. David did neither. Instead, he went together with his men and inquired again of God's answer—seeking God's wisdom and not depending on their own wisdom. David understood a key principle of unity: that if the Spirit had spoken something to him, he would also speak it to his men If he had heard it wrong, now he would hear what the men would. He was willing to go together to unity with God. It is important to note that God does not mind confirming His wisdom to us—and in fact uses unity for us all to hear what is the will of God. Further, God did reinforce that they were to save Keilah, and gave more specific information—that He would deliver the victory. As a result of all hearing God together in unity, they fully understood God's will and were obedient in going to save the town, which they did. Saving the town also had other significant benefits for the men. They were able to once again live a more normal life with prepared food, sleeping in beds, playing games, having fellowship and conversation, and worshiping. They were thrilled that they were able to stay in such a wonderful place.

After a few months, Saul discovered that David and his men

were still in Keilah, and set out to kill them. Keilah was a town surrounded by a mountainous area that provided only one route in and out of the town. Saul reasoned that if he could easily capture David within the town since there was no escape. This moment is another key element in seeking God's will. David might have presumed that since God had given him the victory once and they were living in such a pleasant place, that, of course, He would prevent Saul from coming. Besides, if Saul did attack, the men of Keilah would protect them. However, David made no such assumption. He did not follow simple logic to carry out the next piece of God's will. Instead, he went again to neutrality and sought God's wisdom. He had two significant questions: is Saul coming? Will the men of Keilah hand me over? If God had answered the first question no (even though his information was that Saul was coming), he would have stayed in the town without anxiety. Since God answered yes, he needed to know the answer to the second question. Even though it would seem that, since he had saved the town, these men would save him. God again answered yes, they will hand them over. As a result he understood that God's will was to not stay and fight but rather to leave. This is another key element of our understanding God's will. We cannot assume that just because something happened before that it is God's will again. Each situation is unique. Our role is to completely surrender to God's will and not test Him with our own thoughts of the best way to achieve our desired results. So, David left and Saul stopped the expedition. He was not captured and was preserved as a result following God's will. An important question to con- sider is: since the men never had an opportunity to hand over David, how did God know that they would? This is one of the most amazing characteristics of God—He can play the future in virtual reality. He can see it all play out as if already happened, even though it may never. He can see each event forward based on our decisions. What a privilege this is for us. God sees down the road and knows what will be best for us. Our role is not to presume or decide on our own, but rather to continually seek Him step-by-step. We do this by going to unity together and being always willing to follow what He has to say.

2 Chronicles 20: 1–23:

1 It happened after this that the people of Moab with the people of Ammon, and others with them besides the Ammonites, came to battle against Jehoshaphat. 2 Then some came and told Jehoshaphat, saying, "A great multitude is coming against you from beyond the sea, from Syria; and they are in Hazazon Tamar" (which is En Gedi). 3 And Jehoshaphat feared, and set himself to seek the Lord, and proclaimed a fast throughout all Judah. 4 So Judah gathered together to ask help from the Lord; and from all the cities of Judah they came to seek the Lord. 5 Then Jehoshaphat stood in the assembly of Judah and Jerusalem, in the house of the Lord, before the new court, 6 and said: "O Lord God of our fathers, are You not God in heaven, and do You not rule over all the kingdoms of the nations, and in Your hand is there not power and might, so that no one is able to withstand You? 7 Are You not our God, who drove out the inhabitants of this land before Your people Israel, and gave it to the descendants of Abraham Your friend forever? 8 And they dwell in it, and have built You a sanctuary in it for Your name, saying, 9 'If disaster comes upon us—sword, judgment, pestilence, or famine—we will stand before this temple and in Your presence (for Your name is in this temple), and cry out to You in our affliction, and You will hear and save.' 10 And now, here are the people of Ammon, Moab, and Mount Seir—whom You would not let Israel invade when they came out of the land of Egypt, but they turned from them and did not destroy the —11 here they are, rewarding us by coming to throw us out of Your possession which You have given us to inherit. 12 O our God, will

You not judge them? For we have no power against this great multitude that is coming against us; nor do we know what to do, but our eyes are upon You." 13 Now all Judah, with their little ones, their wives, and their children, stood before the Lord. 14 Then the Spirit of the Lord came upon Jahaziel the son of Zechariah, the son of Benaiah, the son of Jeiel, the son of Mattaniah, a Levite of the sons of Asaph, in the midst of the assembly. 15 And he said, "Listen, all you of Judah and you inhabitants of Jerusalem, and you, King Jehoshaphat! Thus says the Lord to you: 'Do not be afraid nor dismayed because of this great multitude, for the battle is not yours, but God's. 16 Tomorrow go down against them. They will surely come up by the Ascent of Ziz, and you will find them at the end of the brook before the Wilderness of Jeruel. 17 You will not need to fight in this battle. Position yourselves, stand still and see the salvation of the Lord, who is with you, O Judah and Jerusalem!' Do not fear or be dismayed; tomorrow go out against them, for the Lord is with you." 18 And Jehoshaphat bowed his head with his face to the ground, and all Judah and the inhabitants of Jerusalem bowed before the Lord, worshiping the Lord. 19 Then the Levites of the children of the Kohathites and of the children of the Korahites stood up to praise the Lord God of Israel with voices loud and high. 20 So they rose early in the morning and went out into the Wilderness of Tekoa; and as they went out, Jehoshaphat stood and said, "Hear me, O Judah and you inhabitants of Jerusalem: Believe in the Lord your God, and you shall be established; believe His prophets, and you shall prosper." 21 And when he had consulted with the people, he appointed those who should sing to the Lord, and who should praise the beauty of holiness, as they went out before the army and were saying: "Praise the Lord, For His mercy endures forever." 22 Now when they began to sing and to praise, the Lord set ambushes against the people of Ammon, Moab, and Mount

Seir, who had come against Judah; and they were defeated.
23 For the people of Ammon and Moab stood up against the
inhabitants of Mount Seir to utterly kill and destroy them.
And when they had made an end of the inhabitants of Seir,
they helped to destroy one another. 24 So when Judah came
to a place overlooking the wilderness, they looked toward the
multitude; and there were their dead bodies, fallen on the
earth. No one had escaped. 25 When Jehoshaphat and his
people came to take away their spoil, they found among them
an abundance of valuables on the dead bodies, and precious
jewelry, which they stripped off for themselves, more than
they could carry away; and they were three days gathering
the spoil because there was so much. 26 And on the fourth
day they assembled in the Valley of Berachah, for there they
blessed the Lord; therefore the name of that place was called
The Valley of Berachah until this day. 27 Then they returned,
every man of Judah and Jerusalem, with Jehoshaphat in
front of them, to go back to Jerusalem with joy, for the Lord
had made them rejoice over their enemies. 28 So they came
to Jerusalem, with stringed instruments and harps and trum-
pets, to the house of the Lord. 29 And the fear of God was on
all the kingdoms of those countries when they heard that the
Lord had fought against the enemies of Israel. 30 Then the
realm of Jehoshaphat was quiet, for his God gave him rest all
around.

The context here is that Jehoshaphat, as King, has begun to
bring Israel to once again live according to God's command-
ments and seeking His wisdom. He discovers that several
nations have banded together to attack Israel. They are bringing a massive army and since warfare then was primarily one
through which the larger army overwhelmed the smaller one.
Thus, the chance for Israel to defeat this attacking army was
minimal. In today's geography it would be like Egypt and

Jordan and Syria all banding together to attack Israel. Israel would have little hope of victory. Knowing that they lacked power to win this battle, Jehoshaphat called all the leaders and their families together to seek God in unity. He called for a time of prayer and fasting. They exercised James 1: 5—8 and asked for wisdom. They all surrendered their will and stood on the promise that God had already made—that no Army would be able to defeat Israel if they followed God fully and with true hearts. They further understood that they did not have any answers. As a result of them seeking God in unity, God spoke that the battle would not be theirs but God's; go out and stand in battle formation the next day see all that God was about ready to do. There was neither dissension nor argument against what God had spoken, even though it didn't make sense in the natural. All were in unity. They were obedient to God's instructions and went out the next day, praising and believing that what God had personally spoken to them was about ready to happen. It did. The armies that were attacking Israel all fought each other and everyone was killed. God's statement that the battle was His and not theirs was completely true. They did not even have to lift one finger, but just watched.

As a result of the defeat, Israel was able to take all of the enemy's precious goods back to Jerusalem—in fact, there was so much that it took four days to accomplish. (Think about why they had so many material things with them—they expected to easily win and to occupy Israel. They were bringing all of their goods for their new land with them). So, what began as a severe threat to Israel's survival, turned into a blessing. Further, because of the amazing defeat, there was complete rest and peace during Jehoshaphat's reign—another beautiful blessing from God. The key is to seek God in unity. No matter what you are facing, go together to hear God's promises and His solution for your circumstances.

Acts 1: 9–26;

9 *Now when He had spoken these things, while they watched, He was taken up, and a cloud received Him out of their sight.* **10** *And while they looked steadfastly toward heaven as He went up, behold, two men stood by them in white apparel,* **11** *who also said, "Men of Galilee, why do you stand gazing up into heaven? This same Jesus, who was taken up from you into heaven, will so come in like manner as you saw Him go into heaven."* **12** *Then they returned to Jerusalem from the mount called Olivet, which is near Jerusalem, a Sabbath day's journey.* **13** *And when they had entered, they went up into the upper room where they were staying: Peter, James, John, and Andrew; Philip and Thomas; Bartholomew and Matthew; James the son of Alphaeus and Simon the Zealot; and Judas the son of James.* **14** *These all continued with one accord in prayer and supplication, with the women and Mary the mother of Jesus, and with His brothers.* **15** *And in those days Peter stood up in the midst of the disciples (altogether the number of names was about a hundred and twenty), and said,* **16** *"Men and brethren, this Scripture had to be fulfilled, which the Holy Spirit spoke before by the mouth of David concerning Judas, who became a guide to those who arrested Jesus;* **17** *for he was numbered with us and obtained a part in this ministry."* **18** *(Now this man purchased a field with the wages of iniquity; and falling headlong, he burst open in the middle and all his entrails gushed out.* **19** *And it became known to all those dwelling in Jerusalem; so that field is called in their own language, Akel Dama, that is, Field of Blood.)* **20** *"For it is written in the book of Psalms: 'Let his dwelling place be desolate, And let no one live in it'; and, 'Let another take his office.'* **21** *"Therefore, of these men who have accompanied us all the time that the Lord Jesus went in and out among us,* **22**

beginning from the baptism of John to that day when He was taken up from us, one of these must become a witness with us of His resurrection." 23 And they proposed two: Joseph called Barsabas, who was surnamed Justus, and Matthias. 24 And they prayed and said, "You, O Lord, who know the hearts of all, show which of these two You have chosen 25 to take part in this ministry and apostleship from which Judas by transgression fell, that he might go to his own place." 26 And they cast their lots, and the lot fell on Matthias. And he was numbered with the eleven apostles.

The context here is that after the resurrection and Ascension of Jesus, there were now only eleven disciples. They gathered in unity and together sought the Lord on what to do next. They were told to select a new disciple, and that God would provide it to them. They all surrendered their will to the choice, and prayed that God would give them the answer to their question. They selected by lot, knowing that the answer would be God's, and Matthias was selected. There was complete unity—no dissension or division or working to persuade based on their own opinion—rather just seeking God's will.

Acts 2: 1–4:
1 When the Day of Pentecost had fully come, they were all with one accord in one place. 2 And suddenly there came a sound from heaven, as of a rushing mighty wind, and it filled the whole house where they were sitting. 3 Then there appeared to them divided tongues, as of fire, and one sat upon each of them. 4 And they were all filled with the Holy Spirit and began to speak with other tongues, as the Spirit gave them utterance.

The disciples had been instructed to wait in Jerusalem until the power of the Holy Spirit came upon them. It is significant to note that on the day of Pentecost when the Holy Spirit was released, they were all together in unity, praying for the will of the Father. Power comes through unity. There was no dissension—just simple obedience while they prayed in unity, waiting for God to fulfill his promises. As a result they experienced the amazing power of the Holy Spirit coming into each of them, with Peter boldly proclaiming Christ.

Acts 2: 40–47:
40 And with many other words he testified and exhorted them, saying, "Be saved from this perverse generation." 41 Then those who gladly received his word were baptized; and that day about three thousand souls were added to them. 42 And they continued steadfastly in the apostles' doctrine and fellowship, in the breaking of bread, and in prayers. 43 Then fear came upon every soul, and many wonders and signs were done through the apostles. 44 Now all who believed were together, and had all things in common, 45 and sold their possessions and goods, and divided them among all, as anyone had need. 46 So continuing daily with one accord in the temple, and breaking bread from house to house, they ate their food with gladness and simplicity of heart, 47 praising God and having favor with all the people. And the Lord added to the church daily those who were being saved.

The early church fully understood the concept of unity. After over three-thousand came to know Christ at Pentecost through the outpouring of the Holy Spirit and Peter's sermon, they began gathering in small groups in people's homes. They continued to receive the truth from the apostles about what they had personally experienced with Christ and later wrote in the Gospels. As they continued in one accord—unity—they personally experienced many wonders and signs. They saw supernatural things happening all the time as they were experiencing their personal oneness with God. Their hearts were lifted in praise and they found great favor with those that wanted to know about the supernatural things that were happening—coming to hear and then receiving Christ as their Lord and Savior. As they were added, they learned this concept of unity—going to one accord and staying in fellowship - in the Word and in processing truth together. One of the expectations we should hold is that while we are experiencing unity with our spouse, we will be seeing signs and wonders and be in awe of the work of God. He wants to demonstrate that achieving His will is best and none better and is not just naturally good, but supernaturally good. He acts and can change circumstances and bring about His will in mighty and amazing ways. Nothing is too difficult for him and in whatever situation we are facing, we will experience the wonder and the awe of His supernatural work. He desires to draw us up out of our mediocrity and fatalism to a grand life bathed in His amazing power and might—and all through unity.

Acts 4: 1–36:

1 Now as they spoke to the people, the priests, the captain of the temple, and the Sadducees came upon them, 2 being greatly disturbed that they taught the people and preached in Jesus the resurrection from the dead. 3 And they laid hands on them, and put them in custody until the next day, for it was already evening. 4 However, many of those who heard the word believed; and the number of the men came to be about five thousand. 5 And it came to pass, on the next day, that their rulers, elders, and scribes, 6 as well as Annas the high priest, Caiaphas, John, and Alexander, and as many as were of the family of the high priest, were gathered together at Jerusalem. 7 And when they had set them in the midst, they asked, "By what power or by what name have you done this?" **8** *Then Peter, filled with the Holy Spirit, said to them, "Rulers of the people and elders of Israel:* **9** *If we this day are judged for a good deed done to a helpless man, by what means he has been made well,* **10** *let it be known to you all, and to all the people of Israel, that by the name of Jesus Christ of Nazareth, whom you cruci-fied, whom God raised from the dead, by Him this man stands here before you whole.* **11** *This is the 'stone which was rejected by you builders, which has become the chief cornerstone.'* **12** *Nor is there salvation in any other, for there is no other name under heaven given among men by which we must be saved."* **13** *Now when they saw the boldness of Peter and John, and perceived that they were uneducated and untrained men, they marveled. And they realized that they had been with Jesus.* **14** *And seeing the man who had been healed standing with them, they could say nothing against it.* **15** *But when they had commanded them to go aside out of the council, they conferred among themselves,* **16** *saying, "What shall we do to these men? For, indeed, that a notable miracle has been done through them is evident to all who dwell in Jerusalem, and we cannot deny it.* **17** *But so that it spreads no further among the people, let us severely threaten them, that from now on they speak to no man in this name."* **18** *And they called them and commanded them not to speak at all nor teach in the name of Jesus.* **19** *But Peter and John answered and said to them, "Whether it is right in the sight of God to listen to you more than to God, you judge.* **20** *For we cannot but speak the things which we have seen and heard."* **21** *So when they had further threat-ened them, they let them go, finding no way of punishing them, because of the people, since they all glorified God for what had been done.* **22** *For the man was over forty years old on whom this miracle of healing had been performed.*

23 And being let go, they went to their own companions and reported all that the chief priests and elders had said to them. 24 So when they heard that, they raised their voice to God with one accord and said: "Lord, You are God, who made heaven and earth and the sea, and all that is in them, 25 who by the mouth of Your servant David have said: 'Why did the nations rage, And the people plot vain things? 26 The kings of the earth took their stand, And the rulers were gathered together Against the Lord and against His Christ.' 27 "For truly against Your holy Servant Jesus, whom You anointed, both Herod and Pontius Pilate, with the Gentiles and the people of Israel, were gathered together 28 to do whatever Your hand and Your purpose determined before to be done. 29 Now, Lord, look on their threats, and grant to Your servants that with all boldness they may speak Your word, 30 by stretching out Your hand to heal, and that signs and wonders may be done through the name of Your holy Servant Jesus." 31 And when they had prayed, the place where they were assembled together was shaken; and they were all filled with the Holy Spirit, and they spoke the word of God with boldness. 32 Now the multitude of those who believed were of one heart and one soul; neither did anyone say that any of the things he possessed was his own, but they had all things in common. 33 And with great power the apostles gave witness to the resurrection of the Lord Jesus. And great grace was upon them all. 34 Nor was there anyone among them who lacked; for all who were possessors of lands or houses sold them, and brought the proceeds of the things that were sold, 35 and laid them at the apostles' feet; and they distributed to each as anyone had need. 36 And Joses, who was also named Barnabas by the apostles (which is translated Son of Encouragement), a Levite of the country of Cyprus, 37 having land, sold it, and brought the money and laid it at the apostles' feet.

Even after the disciples had been chastised by the Pharisees and told to stop spreading the gospel of Christ, they were not afraid. Rather, they explained that they had no choice but to express what they themselves had experienced. The essence of their Covenant is that we are blessed to be a blessing; and that we are to receive, then and give it away. They gathered together in prayer and raised their voices in unity begging God to continue his miraculous work amongst them and overcome the threats of the Pharisees. As they prayed in unity and spoke the word with boldness together, God continued His supernatural power and fulfillment of His will. Many more believed, enjoying His fellowship of unity. It spread from group to group. They believed in unity, experienced supernatural things in unity, and many others joined this unity. The Father desires for us to lift up our hearts and thinking from the natural to the supernatural—where He is glorified and others will seek to join this work and experience that for themselves. The gospel is not just a philosophy, but a supernatural life of God in His Kingdom.

Acts 10: 1–48:

1 There was a certain man in Caesarea called Cornelius, a centurion of what was called the Italian Regiment, 2 a devout man and one who feared God with all his household, who gave alms generously to the people, and prayed to God always. 3 About the ninth hour of the day he saw clearly in a vision an angel of God coming in and saying to him, "Cornelius!" 4 And when he observed him, he was afraid, and said, "What is it, lord?" So he said to him, "Your prayers and your alms have come up for a memorial before God. 5 Now send men to Joppa, and send for Simon whose surname is Peter. 6 He is lodging with Simon, a tanner, whose house is by the sea. He will tell you what you must do." 7 And when the angel who spoke to him had departed, Cornelius called two of his household servants and a devout soldier from among those who waited on him continually. 8 So when he had explained all these things to them, he sent them to Joppa. 9 The next day, as they went on their journey and drew near the city, Peter went up on the housetop to pray, about the sixth hour. 10 Then he became very hungry and wanted to eat; but while they made ready, he fell into a trance 11 and saw heaven opened and an object like a great sheet bound at the four corners, descending to him and let down to the earth. 12 In it were all kinds of four-footed animals of the earth, wild beasts, creeping things, and birds of the air. 13 And a voice came to him, "Rise, Peter; kill and eat." 14 But Peter said, "Not so, Lord! For I have never eaten anything common or unclean." 15 And a voice spoke to him again the second time, "What God has cleansed you must not call common." 16 This was done three times. And the object was taken up into heaven again. 17 Now while Peter wondered within himself what this vision which he had seen meant, behold, the men who had been sent from Cornelius had made inquiry for Simon's house, and stood before the gate. 18 And they called and asked whether Simon, whose surname was Peter, was lodging there. 19 While Peter thought about the vision, the Spirit said to him, "Behold, three men are seeking you. 20 Arise therefore, go down and go with them, doubting nothing; for I have sent them." 21 Then Peter went down to the men who had been sent to him from Cornelius, and said, "Yes, I am he whom you seek. For what reason have you come?" 22 And they said, "Cornelius the centurion, a just man, one who fears God and has a good reputation among all the nation of the Jews, was divinely instructed by a holy angel to summon you to his house, and to hear words from you." 23 Then he invited them in and lodged them. On the next day Peter went away with them, and some brethren from

Joppa accompanied him. **24** *And the following day they entered Caesarea. Now Cornelius was waiting for them, and had called together his relatives and close friends.* **25** *As Peter was coming in, Cornelius met him and fell down at his feet and worshiped him.* **26** *But Peter lifted him up, saying, "Stand up; I myself am also a man."* **27** *And as he talked with him, he went in and found many who had come together.* **28** *Then he said to them, "You know how unlawful it is for a Jewish man to keep company with or go to one of another nation. But God has shown me that I should not call any man common or unclean.* **29** *Therefore I came without objection as soon as I was sent for. I ask, then, for what reason have you sent for me?"* **30** *So Cornelius said, "Four days ago I was fasting until this hour; and at the ninth hour I prayed in my house, and behold, a man stood before me in bright clothing,* **31** *and said, 'Cornelius, your prayer has been heard, and your alms are remembered in the sight of God.* **32** *Send therefore to Joppa and call Simon here, whose surname is Peter. He is lodging in the house of Simon, a tanner, by the sea. When he comes, he will speak to you.'* **33** *So I sent to you immediately, and you have done well to come. Now therefore, we are all present before God, to hear all the things commanded you by God."* **34** *Then Peter opened his mouth and said: "In truth I perceive that God shows no partiality.* **35** *But in every nation whoever fears Him and works righteousness is accepted by Him.* **36** *The word which God sent to the children of Israel, preaching peace through Jesus Christ—He is Lord of all—* **37** *that word you know, which was proclaimed throughout all Judea, and began from Galilee after the baptism which John preached:* **38** *how God anointed Jesus of Nazareth with the Holy Spirit and with power, who went about doing good and healing all who were oppressed by the devil, for God was with Him.*

39 And we are witnesses of all things which He did both in the land of the Jews and in Jerusalem, whom they killed by hanging on a tree. 40 Him God raised up on the third day, and showed Him openly, 41 not to all the people, but to witnesses chosen before by God, even to us who ate and drank with Him after He arose from the dead. 42 And He commanded us to preach to the people, and to testify that it is He who was ordained by God to be Judge of the living and the dead. 43 To Him all the prophets witness that, through His name, whoever believes in Him will receive remission of sins." 44 While Peter was still speaking these words, the Holy Spirit fell upon all those who heard the word. 45 And those of the circumcision who believed were astonished, as many as came with Peter, because the gift of the Holy Spirit had been poured out on the Gentiles also. 46 For they heard them speak with tongues and magnify God. Then Peter answered, 47 "Can anyone forbid water, that these should not be baptized who have received the Holy Spirit just as we have?" 48 And he commanded them to be baptized in the name of the Lord. Then they asked him to stay a few days.

This is an amazing story of unity and how God works everything together to fulfill His purposes. Cornelius was a Roman centurion (leader of one-hundred soldiers), who had rejected the myths of Roman gods and believed that there was a true God—though he did not know exactly who God was. As he was praying to this unknown God, and Angel appeared to him and said that his prayers have been answered; to send men to Caesarea and find Peter, who was staying there. At the same time, Peter was up on the rooftop of a house praying as he normally did in the afternoon. During his prayer, the Lord revealed to him a vision of all sorts of animals, including those unclean, and told Peter to go ahead and eat this unclean food.

Since this was so contrary to Peter's understanding of the Old Testament, he refused. The vision was given three times and each time Peter said no. (We must note that it is not unusual for God to bring new revelation to us that might challenge our current thinking. It is normal that we would resist this.) To Peter's credit, though he was struggling with the simplicity of this command, he continued to wonder and ponder about what this all meant. As he was pondering, the Spirit told him that some Gentiles were coming to his house to ask him to go with them; and to go. Though he was struggling with the vision, he was quite used to hearing from the Holy Spirit and receiving instruction. He willingly went with these men. As they were walking to Cornelius's home, he continued to ponder the vision and prayed that the Father would reveal all that He was doing. Peter did understand a very important piece of seeking God's will through unity: listen, watch, and wait; ask, seek, and knock. As Peter prayed for wisdom, he knew that the next things that happened would be God speaking to him. He understood that these men were part of God's activity and answering his prayers.

After he arrived at Cornelius's house, he heard the entire story of the Angel appearing before Cornelius and asking him to send for Peter. It was at this moment that it all became clear to Peter—that God was not just talking about food, but about the fact that the gospel had no partiality—it was for everyone, Jews and Gentiles alike. As a result, Peter preached Christ to the Gentiles and the entire household believed, and was filled with the Holy Spirit—and was baptized. God had worked both sides of this issue to bring unity to both. It took hearts to hear, a neutrality to truly seek God's will, and continue to process until God's wisdom was known. He used this process on both sides of listen, watch, wait; and ask, seek, knock to verify in unity with His will. No matter how hard the question was, especially for Peter, God had no trouble answering and revealing His will.

As a result, this amazing moment, turned the world upside down and expanded the gospel to all mankind—all because Cornelius and Peter were willing to walk toward unity until they saw unity. What a beautiful thing.

CHAPTER 9

Psalm 133 . . . There The Lord Commands Blessings

It's very simple. As we come to unity, there—God commands blessing. It is a promise, it will happen, so why would we not want to experience the fullness of God's life. We just need to understand the key principles of this:

1. God hates division—and in fact calls it an abomination. In division, we experience the opposite of a blessing—the consequences of our own choices and failure—certainly mediocrity and definitely not the best.

2. Division is caused by our natural selfishness. Division happens to people who desire their own way and will debate and argue to persuade the others of that way. In fact, because of our selfishness, we cause our own consequences. We are called to deny self and live in the Spirit.

3. Unity is not negotiation or compromise; rather, it is unity with the Spirit. When our spirits say yes when God says yes, we experience tremendous blessings—God's best for us. Unity is possible 100 percent of the time all the time—because the same Spirit is in

all believers, particularly husbands and wives who are always called to go to unity on all decisions—and thus are to stay with it until they do.

4. The basic key to unity is to want to—we each must make a decision that we are not going to make any decisions alone, but only in unity. It is okay to disagree, but each must maintain integrity in the disagreement. Understand that we just do not yet know God's will. We must keep going until we do.

5. To reach unity in the Spirit (remember, not through negotiation or compromise) requires us to learn how to abide in the Vine—walk in the Spirit: in love, in light—always pursuing the truth, and in wisdom—always seeking His will and not our own.

6. When we disagree (remember, it is necessary and valuable to the process) we are to process through the disagreement with honor and respect; and never work to persuade the other to acquiesce to our own desire but to continue in process until we reach unity. There is no time limit, and thus solutions never are to be forced but rather to let the Father reveal His solution—and that comes with unity in the Spirit.

7. We have the privilege of prayer—asking Him for solutions, and being open to the prophetic prayer life where He can reveal new things that we could not possibly know and of things ahead that He will use to guide us to His will.

Since in unity, God commands Blessing—why would we not?

About the Author

Richard T. Case has over 45 years of executive line management experience, both as a senior executive with Fortune 500 companies and as a management consultant to numerous industries and companies. He has also been a featured speaker at numerous conferences and seminars. Mr. Case has received The *Wall Street Journal* Achievement Award, and is listed in *Who's Who in American Business*. Mr. Case holds an MBA degree from the University of Southern California and he also graduated with a seminary Masters degree from Trinity Evangelical Divinity School, summa cum laude.

More resources by Richard T. Case:

The Restored Life

Living the Restored Life

The Remnant

Available wherever fine books are sold!

elevate
publishing

A strategic publisher empowering authors to strengthen their brand.

Visit Elevate Publishing for our latest offerings.
www.elevatepub.com